Slaughterhouse

A play

Norman Robbins

Samuel French – London
New York – Sydney – Toronto – Hollywood

FOR AMATEUR PRODUCTION ENQUIRIES

UNITED KINGDOM AND WORLD EXCLUDING NORTH AMERICA

plays@SamuelFrench-London.co.uk

020 7255 4302/01

Each title is subject to availability from Samuel French,

depending upon country of performance.

CHARACTERS

Edith Cartwright
Caroline Clavers
Douglas Dekker
Bradford Kyle
Freddy Bostock
Lynda Molloy
Tanya Mason
Harriet Bales
Stella Bakewell
Romney Marsh

The action of the play takes place in the Lovecraft Room of "Usher", the great country house owned by ageing horror star, Romney Marsh

ACT I
    SCENE 1   Saturday evening
    SCENE 2   Two hours later

ACT II
    SCENE 1   Early Sunday morning
    SCENE 2   Twenty minutes later

Time: the present

Other full-length plays by Norman Robbins
published by Samuel French

The Late Mrs Early
Nightmare
Pull the Other One
A Tomb with a View
Wedding of the Year

Pantomimes by Norman Robbins
published by Samuel French

Aladdin
Alibaba and the Forty Thieves
Cinderella
The Grand Old Duke of York
Hickory Dickory Dock
Humpty Dumpty
Rumpelstiltzkin
Sing a Song of Sixpence
The Sleeping Beauty
Tom, the Piper's Son
The Wonderful Story of Mother Goose

For
Tom and Isobel Goss
with affection

ACT I

The Lovecraft Room of "Usher", the great country house owned by ageing horror star, Romney Marsh. Saturday evening

The rear wall is dominated by twin french windows looking out on to a broad, walled terrace. Beyond this, thick forest can be glimpsed. Thick drapes and matching pelmets hang at the windows. Between the two windows, an ornate bookcase stands, its fine mesh and glass-fronted shelves crammed with first edition copies of Lovecraft's books. Atop this, a priceless Chinese bowl sits, flanked by display plates of Chinese origin. A carved chair stands at each side of the bookcase. Upstage of the half-panelled wall R, is a thick door leading to the Benson Room, and below this, almost spanning the remainder of the wall, a massive fireplace. On the hearth, gothic fire irons rest, and there is a carved wooden fender. Upstage of the fireplace, a wide bell-pull can be seen. Above the mantel is a huge oil painting of Marsh in the character of the mad Arab, Abdul Alhazred, in turban and ragged robe, and to each side of this, double wall lamps with sandy-coloured shades. On the mantel, a jar of spills, a small oblong wooden box, and assorted photographs in miniature frames. Below the fireplace is a carved high-back chair

The opposite wall has an arched central door, and upstage of this, a small writing desk with blotter, paper, envelopes, etc. A small table lamp atop this provides illumination when needed. Above the desk, a small group of dark paintings in matching frames, and to one side, an internal wall telephone. A ladder-back chair is at the desk, slightly pulled out. Below the door, an oblong table stands, and on it, a large tray holding various decanters and glasses. A thirties standard lamp is downstage of this. Above the table, another framed portrait, this of a middle-aged gypsy woman who bears a striking resemblance to Marsh. Carved chairs flank the table

A large, comfortable settee is just off centre L, angled slightly towards the fire, and a narrow table is behind this. A matching armchair is R, facing front. A small round table is by the L arm of this. An open box of chocolates is on top of this, plus an almost empty sherry glass. The room is thickly carpeted and is lit from a central fitting. Light switches are upstage of the door L, and downstage of the door R.

When the CURTAIN *rises, it is dusk and the last remnants of a spectacular sunset are visible above the trees. This fades as the scene progresses. The fire is unlit, and the room is unlit by artificial means. Edith Cartwright, an angular lady in her late sixties is standing at the window up R gazing out into the grounds. She is smartly, but plainly dressed, and holds a glass of whisky to her chest. On the settee, Caroline Clavers, an attractive but brittle looking woman of thirty is sitting. She wears a sheath dress to which is pinned a large diamond brooch and a diamond bracelet is coiled about her wrist. She is sipping sherry. Beside her, Douglas Dekker, a prosperous looking man of fifty-two sits. He wears a beautifully cut three-piece suit, and holds a glass of whisky*

Douglas (*sipping*) It was a big disappointment to all of us. I mean—we really thought it would *work*. It was a good script. A good cast. Quigley Coppard directing. It should have gone straight into the West End. So what went wrong? (*Shrugging*) *You* tell *me*. (*He drinks*)

Edith (*drily*) In two words, Douggie—it stank. I know for a fact *Born Laughing* got the thumbs down from *five* managements before that raddled old has-been talked you into mounting it as a vehicle for her non-existent talents.

Douglas (*attempting a laugh*) Oh, come on, Edith. Marsha Cochrane's the best comic actress in the country. She's got an incredible sense of humour.

Edith (*turning to him*) Really? I always thought *her* idea of a great gag was to break into a Home for the Blind and flatten out the Braille.

Douglas Well—maybe she *is* a pain in the veritable, but you've got to admit she's still Box Office.

Edith Oh? So why did you close in Torquay? (*She sips at her drink*)

Douglas (*shrugging*) You could stage the Resurrection at Torquay and *still* lose a packet. That's one place *this* production passes by, I can promise you.

Caroline (*drily*) If it ever gets off the ground. (*Frowning*) Is there any chance of having a light on in here, or does the great man only emerge from his tomb in *total* darkness?

Edith glances at her coldly, then moves to the light switch R and flicks it down. The central light goes on

Edith Is that better?

Caroline gives her a thin smile

And by the way, Miss Clavers. When Rom *does* make an appearance, you'd do well to engage brain before mouth. As I'm sure you've already heard, he's not the easiest person in the world to work with. Don't make the mistake of thinking your physical attributes will compensate for lack of intelligence in performance. Anything less than perfection starts him foaming at the mouth. (*Acidly*) Even the fabled Miss Monk found *that* out to her cost. (*She finishes her drink*)

Caroline (*in disbelief*) Not *Mabel* Monk? The American? You're not telling me *she* appeared in a horror film, are you?

Douglas (*uncomfortable*) No, no. Of course not. Not a horror film. It was at Stratford. Back in nineteen sixty. She'd just finished making a film over here and the powers-that-be thought it would be great publicity to team the world's greatest sex-symbol with Britain's biggest box-office draw. (*Sighing*) It was a total disaster. She was three months' pregnant at the time—though nobody knew it but her. What with drink, drugs and

chronic depression . . . plus the fact that she couldn't learn the damn lines,
Rom simply took her apart. She gave two of the worst performances ever
seen at Stratford, then had a nervous breakdown half-way through the
third night and dropped out. (*Quietly*) It was the last time she ever
worked. (*He takes a drink*)

Edith Not *exactly* true. (*She moves to the drinks table for a refill*) When she
got back to the States she spent the next six months or so hidden away in a
private nursing home, having her brain unscrambled. Then Fox made the
mistake of signing her for the remake of *Blood and Sand*. (*She pours a
drink*) They were eight weeks into shooting when she cracked up again
and killed herself. Post-natal depression, I believe they called it. (*She re-
stoppers the decanter*) Of course, the publicity that followed did wonders
for her reputation. To hear the media go on about her now, you'd think
she *invented* Hollywood. (*She moves back upstage* R) Personally, I could
never see what the attraction was. (*She turns to the window and gazes out*)
Excuse me . . . I can see someone else arriving.

She puts down her glass and exits L

Caroline (*glaring after her*) Snotty bitch.

Douglas (*patting her hand*) Oh, you mustn't mind Edith. She can be a bit on
the abrasive side at initial meetings, but she's harmless enough. (*He rises
and crosses to the window* R) Wonder who the new arrival is? Can't be our
leading lady. She's never turned up anywhere on time in her life. (*He peers
out*) No. Definitely not Tanya. Not her style at all.

Caroline (*surprised*) Tanya Mason?

Douglas (*nodding*) She's replaced Phillipa Jordan as Lady Millicent. Only
fixed it up yesterday. They've extended Phillipa's run in New York till
September.

Caroline Lucky Phillipa. Who else is coming? The entire company?

Douglas Hmm? Oh, no. No. (*He turns away from the window*) Just a select
few according to Edith. Rom's never been one for playing the gracious
host. As a matter of fact I was quite surprised when he suggested we came
down here. There aren't many can claim they've set foot in *this* place since
he moved in. It's like a damn fortress.

Caroline Is he all there, do you think? I mean—all this. (*She indicates
around her*) It's crazy. Like something out of one of his films.

Douglas (*laughing*) It *is*. The exterior's an exact copy of the one they
knocked up for *The House of Usher*—hence the name. When Rom found
the place last year it was just an old ruin, but it caught his fancy and he
had it re-built the way it is now. Cost him a fortune, I hear, but it's what
he wanted. The King of Horror's House of Nightmares.

Caroline (*distastefully*) Nightmare's right. You should see the room they've
put me in. Overlooking a *graveyard*, for God's sake.

Douglas (*smiling*) Not a real one, though. Last used in *Revenge of the Ghoul*
if memory serves me right. Courtesy of Pinewood Studios.

Caroline Looks real enough to me. It's absolutely sick. The first thing I did
was to close the curtains. I can do very well without seeing *that* every time
I walk into the room.

Bradford Kyle strides into the room through the door L. *Blessed with devastating good looks, he admits to forty-seven years of age, and is dressed in expensive jacket, sweater and slacks. He affects a high camp manner*

Bradford (*expansively*) Douggie, darling. (*He crosses to him and grabs his hand*) Lovely to see you again. How's Angela? Still living together, or have you been a good boy and made an honest woman of her?

Douglas (*stiffly*) Hallo, Brad. I didn't expect to see *you* here. I thought you were still in Paris. (*He frees himself*)

Bradford (*making a moue*) Don't remind me, darling. Utter disaster. Two days after we arrived there, the little queen ran off with a kitchen porter— and my Rolex oyster. (*He notices Caroline*) Hallo, darling. (*Realizing*) Oh. You're not Douggie's new popsie, are you? Don't tell me I've gone and put my foot in it again. (*He holds out his hand*) Bradford Kyle. Star of Stage, Screen, and you name it. (*He smiles warmly*)

Caroline (*extending her hand*) Hallo. Caroline Clavers. I'm playing Zoe.

They brush fingers

Bradford (*to Douglas*) Bit of a coincidence you being here, isn't it? Actually I was coming in to see you on Monday, but I thought I'd drop in on Rom first. I heard you were looking for someone to play Rudolph, or whatever his name is, in the new play, so I dropped everything and took the first plane back. You've not cast it yet, have you?

Douglas (*hesitantly*) Well—no, as a matter of fact we haven't. We're seeing people on Monday and Wednesday, but——

Bradford (*firmly*) Cancel them, darling. Your Rudolph stands before you in all his pristine whatsit. (*He strikes a pose*) Oh, I know it's not the *lead*, but the chance of working with Rom again ... and in his first stage play for *years* ... well ... you know *me*. I'd walk starkers down Regent Street for a chance like that. Can I do it?

Douglas (*moving towards the fireplace*) It's not quite as simple as that, Brad. (*Glancing at Caroline*) Perhaps you'd better come and see me at the office. Ask your agent to make an appointment.

Bradford Oh, there's no need to bring George into it. We can fix this up between us. Old pals, eh? Why pay commission when you can arrange things yourself? You haven't a spare script handy, by the way? Give me a chance to run the old peepers over it before the read-through.

Douglas I'm afraid not. (*Throwing another look at Caroline*) Look—Brad. I—er—I don't think this is a good time for talking. We're down here at Rom's invitation, and you know what he's like for his privacy.

Bradford You don't have to worry about *Rom*. He'll be delighted to see me. Didn't I share billing with him in *Spawn of the Zombie Queen*?

Edith enters L *in time to hear this*

Edith (*tartly*) No-one *shares* billing with Rom. And what are *you* doing here?

Bradford (*warmly*) Edith, darling. It's been *ages*. Missed your friendly face.

Edith I asked you a question? How did you get past the gate? I gave strict orders that *no-one* could be admitted unless their name was on the guest list. *Yours* was conspicuously absent.

Bradford Well, of course it was, darling. I didn't know I was coming myself till this afternoon. When I pulled up in the jolly old motor car, the fellow asked if I were Mr Bostock, so I told him I was. He let me in without a murmur.

Edith (*annoyed*) You had no right to say anything of the kind. Now I suggest you clamber right back into your jolly old *motor car* and leave here at once. And the next time you decide to gatecrash a private gathering, I'd appreciate it if you'd make your entrance through the main door like everyone else, and not go sneaking around the back. Is that clear?

The telephone rings. At once she moves to it and answers

Yes? (*She listens*) Yes. That's quite correct. Let him through. The other gentleman was an imposter. (*She listens*) No, no. There's no need for that. He'll be leaving again in a moment. (*She listens*) That's quite all right. It wasn't your fault. Mr Kyle is an *expert* deceiver. (*She replaces the receiver*) Freddy Bostock's here. (*To Bradford*) I'll see you to your car.

Bradford Oh, come on Edith. You can't throw me out before I've had the guided tour. I've been dying to look round the place ever since he bought it, but never had the chance.

Edith Perhaps some other time. But for the moment ... (*She indicates the door*)

Bradford (*laughing*) What *is* this? I mean—why the hurry to get rid of me? I'm one of Rom's friends, for God's sake.

Edith If Rom had wanted you here, he'd have invited you. Now please leave.

Bradford (*firmly*) Sorry to disappoint you, darling, but I'm not taking a step till Rom himself tells me to go. Understand?

Edith (*after a slight pause*) Very well. If that's your attitude. But don't say you weren't warned.

Edith exits L, looking grim

Caroline Did I detect a whiff of sulphur as milady made her exit?

Bradford (*sitting beside her, all charm again*) The trouble with Edith is, she thinks she's the Zombie Queen herself. How I'd love to see *her* go up in the sacred flames. (*He grins*) So you're playing Zoe, are you? And what do you think of the script? Good, is it?

Douglas Fantastic. Another *Mousetrap*.

Caroline (*thoughtfully*) It's a typical Romney Marsh vehicle. Not too much for anyone else, but I've a fairly good suicide scene in Act Two. To be honest though, I can't see why he wants to do it. He's playing Solomons— that's the antique dealer—and he's got fewer lines than I have. It doesn't make sense.

Bradford I shouldn't worry about that. We're not in rehearsal yet. By the time Rom's finished, we'll be lucky to have a dozen lines each. You

wouldn't believe the changes he made to *The Bellringer* on his last tour.
Even the writer couldn't recognize it.

Caroline (*sharply*) Well, I hope he doesn't start cutting *my* lines. I'm not
some two-bit rep actress, you know.

Bradford (*innocently*) I think you should *tell* him that, darling. He does tend
to go overboard when he's in a creative mood. (*Easily*) As for myself,
well, I'm content to pick up the crumbs he scatters when he's finished the
meal. And speaking of meals. You've not eaten yet, have you? I'm
absolutely starving.

Douglas I expect there'll be dinner when the rest of them arrive, but I
wouldn't count on being included in on it, if I were you. Look, Brad. Why
don't you slip away before Rom comes down? I'll have a word with him
about the part, I promise. If he knows you're interested . . .

Bradford (*smiling*) That's all right, Douggie. I don't mind asking him
myself. We do go back a long way, you know.

Freddy Bostock enters L. *He is an intense looking young man of thirty,
bespectacled and wearing a suit that hangs oddly on his slim frame*

Douglas (*warmly*) Freddy. Come in. (*Indicating Caroline*) Caroline Clavers
. . . who's playing Zoe, and er——

Freddy (*quickly*) Bradford Kyle. (*He smiles nervously*) I'd recognize *you*
anywhere Mr Kyle. I saw you in *Bitter Harvest* five times. (*He extends his
hand*)

Bradford (*flattered*) Did you? (*He rises*) Not exactly my greatest role, but it
paid well. (*He laughs and takes hold of Freddy's hand*) Of course, I'm a lot
more choosey about roles these days. Only accept the cream, so to speak.
That's why I'm looking forward to playing Rudolph. You *do* see me as
Rudolph, don't you?

Freddy (*trying to free his hand*) Pardon? (*Realizing*) Oh. It's *Rupert*,
actually. Rupert Collison. (*Finally he gets his hand free*) Well . . . er . . . I
don't know. I mean—If Mr *Dekker* thinks it's all right, that's fine by me. I
mean—an actor of *your* standing. It'd be marvellous. Yes.

Bradford (*pleased*) I *knew* you'd agree. (*To Douglas*) You see? Straight
from the horse's mouth. (*He sits next to Caroline and grins at her
cheerfully*)

Douglas (*uncomfortably*) Can I get you a drink, Freddy?

Freddy I wouldn't say no to a cup of tea. (*Slightly embarrassed*) Haven't
had a thing since I left London.

Bradford I wouldn't mind a cup of tea myself. Keep our brilliant young
author company, eh? (*He beams at Freddy*)

Douglas glares at Bradford and reaches for the bell-pull

No, no. Don't ring. I'll go. (*Archly*) Give me a chance to have a quick
snoop before Edith turns the dogs loose on me. (*He rises*)

Caroline (*sharply*) Dogs? What dogs?

Bradford (*surprised*) Haven't you *seen* them, darling? They're in cages
round the back. Slavering great Dobermanns with very unattractive teeth.
Absolutely dozens of them.

Caroline (*uneasily*) He won't have them in the house, will he? I'm not very fond of dogs.

Douglas I don't think there's much chance of that. Rom's not too keen on dogs himself. (*He frowns*) Can't think why he'd be keeping Dobermanns.

Bradford He isn't. They all belong to Edith. She's training them to rip unwanted guests apart. (*He rolls his eyes*) I'll get that tea.

Bradford exits L

Douglas (*to the others*) Sorry about that. He's a good actor, but he does tend to overstep the boundaries from time to time. He'd be totally wrong for Rupert. And Rom won't even consider it. I can promise you.

Freddy (*slightly embarrassed*) He certainly seems different *off*-stage. Not a bit like I imagined he'd be.

Caroline (*drily*) You live and learn, don't you?

Douglas (*quietly*) Don't let the act fool you. There's more to Brad than meets the eye. (*More briskly*) But sit down, Freddy. Take the weight off your feet. (*He indicates the armchair*)

Freddy (*moving to the chair and sitting*) Thanks. (*He looks around*) Some place, this. Must have cost a fortune.

Douglas Yes.

Freddy (*after a slight pause*) I'm not the last, am I? I mean—I've not kept you waiting?

Douglas Not at all. Still one more to come. The others arrived about a quarter of an hour ago. Still upstairs, I think.

Freddy And Mr Marsh. Romney, that is. Have you seen *him* yet?

Caroline Neither fang nor claw. And *I'm* starting to get a little cheesed off with all this waiting about. Yes, we all know he's a big star, but lesser mortals have private lives too. If it was so desperately important to have a read-through before rehearsal began, why couldn't we have had it in London? My fiancé wasn't exactly pleased at having his weekend arrangements ruined because *I* had to come down here.

Douglas (*soothingly*) I appreciate it was short notice, but it *is* for the good of the play. Rom's a little concerned about the ending of Act One, and wants to try out a few ideas *now* instead of wasting valuable rehearsal time, later. Something I agree with entirely.

Freddy (*anxiously*) It's nothing drastic is it? I mean . . . I tried to keep it as tight as I could.

Douglas (*quickly*) No, no. As far as I know, it's all very minor, but if it's ironed out now, we've got a huge hit on our hands.

Caroline (*muttering*) First time *I've* come across something like this in the professional theatre.

Douglas (*smiling*) Well . . . it's the way Rom likes to work, so we have to indulge him, don't we?

Lynda Molloy, a flamboyant lady of forty-five, enters L, *wearing a striking evening gown*

Lynda (*breezily*) Hallo, darlings. So this is where you're hiding yourselves, is it? (*She crosses to Douglas*)

Douglas Lynda. We were wondering what was keeping you. Now we *know*.
Lynda (*kissing him lightly on the cheek*) Do you like it? (*She twirls around*)
Tell the truth, now.
Douglas You look marvellous.
Lynda (*laughing*) Designed it for Carla Michaels, but I loved it so much I
decided to keep it for my very own. (*She turns to the others*) Well? Aren't
you going to introduce us, Douggie, or do we have to do it ourselves?
Douglas I'm sorry. Of course. Caroline Clavers. (*He indicates her*) Freddy
Bostock. Meet Lynda Molloy, my favourite designer.
Lynda (*laughing*) Liar. (*To Caroline*) Weren't you Virginia Thing in that
hysterical sit-com, *Bright as a Button?*
Caroline (*preening*) Yes. Virginia *Dawson*. They're doing another series
later in the year, but I'm not sure I'll be back with them yet. The usual
argument over money, of course. Not to mention the billing.
Lynda (*sitting on the settee*) I know. It's a constant fight for recognition,
isn't it? I still have the same trouble myself. No-one wants to pay a
fraction of what you're *really* worth. (*Raising her voice and looking at
Douglas with a smile*) Including certain theatrical managers who are
standing not two hundred miles away from here.
Douglas (*affecting deafness*) Pardon? Pardon?
Lynda (*to Freddy*) I *love* the play, Freddy—I *can* call you that, can't I?
Freddy Please.
Lynda I've got the designs upstairs in my room. I'll bring them down later
and we can got through them. (*Smiling*) What on earth gave you the idea
for it? The play, I mean. It could have been written for Rom.
Freddy It *was*, actually. I think I've seen every film he's ever made, so I've
been able to use all his mannerisms and speech patterns in the character of
Solomons.
Lynda That *last* scene should have them on the edge of their seats. It's a
marvellous twist. Totally unexpected.
Douglas Where's Stella? Not feeling shy, is she?
Lynda Don't worry. She'll be down shortly. She's just putting a few
finishing touches to her make-up. When she walks through that door,
she's going to make you jump out of your skins.
Douglas (*easily*) I don't think I like the sound of that.
Lynda (*laughing*) It's nothing frightful. Just a little idea I had. But I wanted
to see your reactions.
Caroline Who's Stella? Or am I being stupid?
Douglas Stella Bakewell. She's playing Cassandra. Can I get you a drink,
Lynda? I'm going to help *myself* to another.
Lynda Divine man. I'll have a whisky, please.

Douglas crosses to the drinks table

Douglas Caroline?
Caroline I thought you'd never ask. (*She hands him her empty glass*)

Douglas pours the drinks

Lynda Has anyone seen Rom, yet? I was hoping to have a quick word with him before I unveiled the set designs, but Edith said he couldn't be disturbed unless the sky fell down.

Tanya Mason sweeps into the room through the door L. *She is a voluptuous woman of fifty-seven, and is every inch a star. Immaculate in dress and coiffure, and dripping with expensive jewellery. She is followed by Bradford*

Tanya And fall it shall, dears, if I don't get a bloody drink within the next few seconds.
Lynda (*warmly*) Tanya.

She stands to greet her, and they brush cheeks. Freddy gapes then rises, whilst Caroline views her shrewdly. Douglas stops pouring

Tanya Darling.
Douglas So you finally made it.
Tanya Sod the pleasantries and fill me a glass, dear. (*To Freddy*) No need to stand, precious. Just treat me like you would any other international star. (*She laughs*) What a journey. Remind me never to buy a house in the country.

Freddy sits again. Tanya moves to the fireplace to dominate the room. Douglas continues pouring

(*Giving a short laugh*) House. Dracula's Castle, more like it. Complete with moat, drawbridge and fake piranha fish.
Douglas Not fake, Tanya. The *real thing*. (*He carries her drink to her*)
Tanya (*laughing loudly*) You're joking. (*To the others*) He's joking, isn't he? (*To Douglas*) You're *joking*. (*She takes the drink*)
Douglas 'Fraid not. According to Edith, there's at least two hundred of them swimming around down there. Harrods had them flown in especially.
Tanya (*shrieking with laughter*) He's gone mad. Flipped his lid completely. Piranha fish in darkest England? What does he feed them on? Door-to-door salesmen? (*She takes a drink*)
Bradford Out-of-work actors, if you ask me. We'd better be very nice to him this weekend, or we'll all be down there practising our breast stroke.
Tanya Oh, shut up, Brad. They didn't tell me *you* were in this ghastly play.

Douglas, Caroline and Lynda look embarrassed

Bradford Not yet, precious, but I'm working on it. (*Indicating Freddy*) This is the author, by the way. Freddy Bostock. (*He grins*)
Tanya Ouch. (*To Freddy*) Only joking, darling. It's a *lovely* play, really. (*Looking around*) So this is "Usher". I must admit the rooms seem spacious enough. I'm not sure I approve of the paintings though. There's something obscene about having one's own image peering down at you when you're trying to relax. (*She turns to look at the painting over the fireplace*) Oh, I suppose I could live with that one, though. It *was* one of his better roles.

Harriet Bales appears in the doorway L. *She is fifty-two, neatly, but plainly dressed, and carries a tray with tea things. As she moves into the room to place the tray on the table, Stella Bakewell follows her in. She is a stunning blond, dressed in a summer frock that would not have been out of place in nineteen-sixty, though obviously modern. As she moves behind the settee, to* c *there is a general reaction*

Douglas (*stunned*) My God.
Stella (*breathily*) Hallo, baby.

Both Tanya and Harriet turn to see her. The whisky glass drops from Tanya's hand and Harriet steps back, mouth gaping. All the others react

Douglas (*staring at Stella*) Wha——(*Angrily*) What the *hell* do you think you're playing at? Are you out of your *mind*?
Lynda (*rising*) What's wrong? What is it?
Douglas (*to Stella*) Is this your idea of a *joke*?

Lynda stares at Douglas speechless as he glares at Stella

Coming in here like that. Haven't you any sense at all?
Stella (*stunned and scared*) What have I done? What's wrong?
Douglas (*recovering himself slightly*) Of all the damn stupid tricks to pull. If Rom had been here . . . (*He shakes his head*)
Lynda (*baffled*) I don't understand.
Douglas (*incredulously*) Don't understand?
Bradford (*sharply*) Of course she doesn't. How could she? She'd only have been a kid at the time. (*To Lynda*) Rom and Mabel didn't exactly hit it off, sweetie. There are those who say she'd never have killed herself if she hadn't had the misfortune to work with him. *Now* does the dawn start to break?
Lynda (*stunned*) Oh, my God. No wonder you all looked as though you'd been turned to stone. I'd no idea. (*To Stella*) Quick. Back upstairs and get into your own things. And don't let anyone see you.

Stella stumbles hurriedly from the room, on the verge of tears

Harriet (*with an effort*) I've brought the tea. Would you like me to pour, or will you help yourselves?
Bradford We'll help ourselves. Thanks.

Harriet exits L

Douglas (*to Tanya*) Are you all right, Tanya? You're white as a sheet.
Tanya (*forcing a smile*) I'm fine. Fine. It was just the shock. Seeing her standing there. (*She picks up the fallen glass*)
Lynda (*anxiously*) I'd no idea. Honestly, I hadn't. I mean—you all know how much I idolized Mabel. (*She sits again*) When I read the script I thought the character of Cassandra seemed to cry out for Mabel Monk, and as Stella faintly resembled her, I came up with that outfit. I thought you'd be ecstatic.
Tanya (*drily*) You're sure you haven't a touch of Mrs Danvers running through your veins, darling?
Freddy Who?
Bradford The mad housekeeper in *Rebecca*. It's a Daphne du Maurier

thing, and she pulls the same kind of stunt with the new wife. Gets her to dress up in the dead one's clothes and scares the life out of hubby and co.

Freddy Oh. Yes. I think I saw the film once.

Bradford moves to the tea things and begins to pour

Lynda (*awkwardly*) Look. I'd appreciate it if we kept this to ourselves. Don't blame Stella. She was only doing what I'd asked her to. I'll apologize to her, of course.

Douglas (*nodding*) I think I owe her an apology, too. It was just a bit of a shock to see her there. Looking like that. As though she'd just stepped off the set.

Bradford carries a cup of tea over to Freddy

Caroline (*sitting beside Lynda*) Funny, isn't it? That's the second time in fifteen minutes Mabel Monk's name has cropped up. We were talking about her just before you came in.

Lynda Oh?

Bradford (*crossing back to the table*) In that case, you'd better mention her a third time, darlings, and get it out of your system. The name's taboo and *verboten* if Rom's in the vicinity.

Lynda But what happened? I mean—she seemed nice enough to me.

Caroline (*looking at her curiously*) You met her?

Lynda Well ... fleetingly. I was only a schoolgirl at the time and she was over here filming *Hallo, Baby* at Bray Studios. I spotted her in the foyer of the Savoy Hotel signing autographs and naturally I wanted one, too, but I didn't have my book with me. She took a snapshot out of her evening bag and autographed the back of that. I treasured it for years. You can imagine how devastated I was when she died.

Tanya (*drily*) You wouldn't have been so devastated if you'd had to *work* with her. She was the most self-centred, over-sexed little trollop I've ever come across. And believe me, I've been around a *long* time.

Bradford I know, darling. You did the cabaret at The Last Supper, didn't you? (*He sips at his tea*)

Tanya I did *Hallo, Baby* with her, and that was an experience and a half. As long as it wore trousers, *nothing* was safe. Isn't that right, Douggie? And age was no barrier. She'd sleep with anything from eight to eighty.

Douglas Let's drop the subject, shall we? We've got far more important things to discuss right now. That all ended thirty years ago.

Tanya (*oddly*) Did it? I wonder.

A strained silence falls. Bradford puts down his cup

Bradford (*brightly*) Anyone for tennis?

Everyone looks at him in a puzzled manner

I've always wanted to say that line in a play, haven't you? Conjures up such a lovely *image*. An English weekend in high Summer. Birds twittering. Strawberry jam, buttered scones, and the exhilarating thwack of a tennis ball on stretched strings. (*He glances out of the window*) And what do *we* get. Billowing fog.

Tanya Fog? (*She glances out of the window*) My God, he's right. Look at it.
Douglas But that's ridiculous. The forecast never said anything about fog.
Bradford Well there it is, dearie. Thicker than pea soup and simply rolling in.
Freddy (*philosophically*) At least we all got here before it came down.
Bradford Yes. And it's just in time to ensure little me will have to stay for dinner. They wouldn't dare toss me out in this lot, would they? (*He glances at his watch*) What *is* keeping Rom?

Edith stalks into the room L *and gives a frosty smile*

Edith If you'd care to follow me to the dining-room, we'll be eating in a few minutes. (*She turns to leave*)
Lynda I'll see if Stella's ready.

Lynda exits L

Tanya Will Rom be joining us, Edith? I must say I'm rather surprised he hasn't seen fit to welcome any of his guests. Particularly *me*.
Edith (*turning back*) He has been rather busy this afternoon, Tanya. There's been a great deal to do. But don't worry. He'll certainly be in his usual place at the table. Now if you wouldn't mind.

Edith turns and exits

The others follow her out and the room is finally empty

A moment later Romney Marsh enters the room, R, *a curious expression on his face. He is sixty-seven years old, slightly stooped, and gaunt. His hair is dyed black and pasted slickly to his skull and he wears evening suit and black patent leather shoes. Crossing to the desk he picks up the telephone receiver and stabs out a two-digit number. After a moment he speaks quietly into the receiver*

Romney Gatehouse? . . . This is Mr Marsh. The last of my guests have arrived and no-one else is expected. You have precisely five minutes to leave the grounds before the security fences are charged, and I shall expect to see you Monday morning sharp, together with the dog handlers as we discussed. In the interest of your *own* safety, I would urge you not to forget them. Have a pleasant weekend. (*He puts the receiver down and narrows his eyes*) Caught. Like rats in a trap. (*He gives a tight smile of utter malice*)

He exits L *into the hall*

The Curtain *falls*

Scene 2

The same. Later that evening

The half-empty sherry glass has been removed from the small table, the other glasses and the tea things have also been removed. The drapes at both windows are drawn. On the table behind the settee, a tray holding coffee pot, sugar bowl, cream jug, etc., and on various flat surfaces, tiny coffee cups and saucers stand discarded

Marsh sits in the armchair, cradling a glass of brandy, a play manuscript at his feet. Freddy sits on the upstage end of the settee, manuscript on his knee, scribbling away. Caroline sits next to him, clutching her open manuscript, and Stella, in a skirt and blouse and re-applied make-up, sits on the chair below the fireplace, coffee cup in hand, and manuscript beside her. Edith and Douglas stand by the bookcase, quietly chatting. Each holds a glass of whisky. There is no sign of the others

Romney ... then when the door opens, Cassandra's body is seen only by Rupert. Do you understand what I mean?

Freddy (*looking up*) So we lose Zoe's line "My God, she's been murdered", plus the rest of that page, and pick up on Rupert's line, "It's Solomons. What are we going to do now?" et cetera?

Romney Exactly. (*He picks up a chocolate and pops it into his mouth*)

Caroline And what about *my* line? The one about *her* being the second one to die? If I haven't seen her, how can I say it? It wouldn't make sense.

Marsh stops chewing and looks at her

Romney Then the solution should be obvious, Miss Clavers. You *don't* say the line. (*He finishes his chocolate and sips his brandy*)

Caroline (*protesting*) But it's my last one in that scene. If you're cutting that, and the whole chunk after it, I may as well not be there at all.

Romney (*in feigned surprise*) Oh? (*Sweetly*) So do we take it you don't intend to *act* for the rest of the scene?

Caroline Well, of course I shall. But I'd like something to act *with*. I don't want to be left standing there like a spare part.

Romney (*reasonably*) But that's exactly what you *are*, my dear. A spare part. Unless I'm very much mistaken, the writer of this script — and you'll correct me if I'm wrong, Mr Bostock — intended the character of *Solomons* to be the central one. *I*, Miss Clavers, am playing Solomons. You — and again, correct me if I'm wrong — have been engaged to play a *minor* role as one of my victims. A role which in view of your reading tonight, would seem to be far in excess of your meagre talents, don't you agree?

Caroline (*stunned*) I — I *beg* your pardon.

Edith and Douglas look at them

Romney (*voice hardening*) No, no, my dear. It's not *my* pardon you should be begging. It's the pardon of this young man here (*indicating Freddy*) who has spent a considerable time constructing his excellent drama only to see it mangled by a so-called actress who would obviously have insurmountable difficulty making sense of a domestic shopping list.

Caroline (*outraged*) How *dare* you speak to me like that? (*She stands angrily*) How dare you?

Romney (*waving a hand in dismissal*) Sit down, woman. Even your outrage lacks belief. Drama school indignation at its pathetic worst. (*To Douglas*) I can't work with this creature. Find a replacement.

Caroline (*hotly*) Don't *bother* yourself. I wouldn't work with this repulsive old monster for an Oscar. For your information, Mr high-and-mighty Marsh, my upbringing was strictly *Kosher*—and *Ham* is something I can well live without.

She storms out of the room, L

Douglas (*heavily*) Rom …

Romney (*easily*) It's all right. No need to apologize. Forget it. You saw for yourself. The woman can't even make a decent exit. (*To Freddy*) Don't worry. We'll find a *real* actress to play Zoe. (*He puts his glass down and turns to Stella*) You. Stand up.

Stella stiffens, face frozen with apprehension, then rises nervously. Marsh regards her thoughtfully

(*Slowly*) It's possible. Possible. (*He nods to himself*) There seems to be a vestige of brain inside that head of yours.

Douglas (*realizing*) But she's already playing Cassandra.

Romney A nothing part. Find someone else for it. She plays Zoe. (*To Stella*) Can you learn it?

Stella (*taken aback*) I think so. (*She nods*)

Romney (*snapping*) I didn't ask you to *think*. I asked if you could learn it?

Stella (*gulping*) Yes, Mr Marsh.

Romney Good. We'll run through the first scene tomorrow. Without books.

Stella opens her mouth to speak

Without books.

Stella (*taking a deep breath*) Yes, Mr Marsh.

Romney (*to Freddy*) You see? How easy it is to solve the major problems. We now have our Zoe and the minor problem of Cassandra will be solved early next week. Isn't that so, Douglas?

Douglas Yes, Rom.

Romney (*re-fixing his gaze on Stella*) Is something wrong?

Stella (*gulping*) No, Mr Marsh.

Romney Then why are you still here? Do you learn your lines by thought transference, perchance?

Stella No, Mr Marsh.

Stella hurries from the room, L

Romney Actresses. (*He selects another chocolate and pops it in his mouth*)

Douglas I'll go and have a word with Caroline.

Romney (*sharply*) No. There's something I want to discuss with you.

Edith begins to move towards the door L

Both of you.

Edith stops and looks at him

Where's Tanya?

Edith Up in her room, I expect.

Romney Call her.

Edith (*glancing at her watch*) It's a quarter to eleven.

Romney (*snarling*) If I'd wanted to know the time, I'd have looked at my watch.

Edith (*quietly*) Yes. Of course. I'll call her now. (*She crosses to the phone and punches out a number*)

Romney (*to Freddy*) You've made notes of all we discussed, Freddy?

Freddy I think s——(*Remembering who he is dealing with*) I mean—yes, sir. I've got them all. Every last one.

Romney (*smiling*) Good. Then you'll have the new version ready for me after breakfast, eh? (*He selects another chocolate and pops it into his mouth*)

Freddy looks at him in dismay

Edith (*on the phone*) Rom would like to see you in the Lovecraft room at once. (*Pause*) Thank you. (*She replaces the receiver*) She'll be right down.

Romney Good. Now tell Mrs Bales to come and clear away these things. (*He indicates the coffee cups, etc.*) The place looks like a pigsty.

Edith moves towards the door L

No. Wait. I want you here. Perhaps Mr Bostock wouldn't mind? (*He looks enquiringly at Freddy*)

Freddy Er—no. Of course not.

He rises and exits L

Romney Sit down. Both of you.

Douglas and Edith exchange glances, then Edith moves to the settee and sits. Douglas moves to the lower end of the fireplace, but remains standing

Douglas (*clearing his throat*) I wish you hadn't done that, Rom. Upset Caroline. She *has* signed a contract and if she wants to make something of it, we could be in big trouble with Equity.

Romney (*drily*) Why should *we* be in trouble? *She* walked out on *us*, remember? You all heard her. Quit because we'd cut a few lines from her part. Do you really think Equity would take up her case in the face of four independent witnesses swearing to this? (*He waves his hand dismissively*)

Douglas It wasn't like that at all. You insulted her professional dignity.

Romney (*coldly*) Dignity, perhaps. Professional, never. Besides—I'm sure no-one here will have any recollection of such an event. *Will they?*

There is silence

Then there'll be no problems with Equity, I assure you.

Edith But we *do* have another problem. I assume that's what you want to talk about? Bradford Kyle.

Romney On the contrary. There is no problem with Brad. If he wants the part, he shall have it. I know I can rely on him.

The door L, *opens and Harriet enters*

(*Brusquely*) Yes?
Harriet I've come for the things, sir.

He gives her a nod. She begins to collect up the coffee things, piling them on to the tray with the coffee pot, etc.

Edith If you'll pardon my saying so, I don't think Brad's the ideal choice for this. In *my* opinion —
Romney When I *want* your opinion, Edith, I'll give it to you. How often do I have to tell you that *I* make the final decision on casting my shows?
Douglas I'm sorry, Rom. But I agree with Edith. Brad's a "name". He commands a big salary and the role of Rupert's hardly more than a juve lead. Hundreds of actors would play the part for a fraction of what we'd have to pay him.
Romney Hundreds of actors would also play Solomons for a fraction of *my* salary. But if you hired *them*, you wouldn't have *me*, would you? Now stop raising stupid objections and arrange for his contract.

Harriet picks up the tray and prepares to leave the room

Tanya enters L

Tanya You wanted to see me?

Harriet exits L

Tanya glances at her as they cross

Romney (*brusquely*) Close the door.

A flicker of surprise crosses her face then she turns and closes the door

Sit down. (*He indicates the settee*)

Tanya moves to it and sits

Tanya Well?
Romney (*after a short silence*) Am I supposed to tremble in my shoes? Call in the police to protect me, or barricade myself behind my own doors? Is this what I'm expected to do? Eh? (*He looks at each of them in turn*)

The trio exchange puzzled looks

(*Testily*) Well? Why doesn't someone answer me?
Douglas If we knew what you were talking about, it would make things a lot easier.
Romney (*angrily*) Do you take me for a fool? (*He stands*) Did you really think I'd have no idea that one of you was responsible?
Tanya Responsible for what?

Romney glares at them, then crosses to the desk, opens a drawer and takes out a large brown envelope

Romney Responsible for *these*.

He shakes the envelope violently between Edith and Tanya. Six yellowing newspaper clippings fall from the envelope. Some have photographs with the story. Both Edith and Tanya pick up a cutting

Douglas What are they?

Tanya (*oddly*) Press cuttings. On Mabel Monk.

Romney Or more specifically, on the *suicide* of Mabel Monk.

Douglas (*moving to the settee*) Let me see.

Edith passes her cutting to him. He reads it quickly then takes Tanya's and glances at that. He picks up the rest and skims through them quickly

(*Puzzled*) Where did you get these?

Romney (*moving towards the fireplace*) I received them in the mail. The first one, Monday last, and the final one this morning. Isn't that obvious? Can't you read the messages scrawled across them?

Douglas (*sorting out the clippings and reading*) Five days. Four days. Three days. Two days. Tomorrow. *Today*. (*He looks up*)

Edith (*frowning*) Sounds like a warning.

Romney (*snarling*) Of course it's a warning. But a warning of *what*?

Tanya Obviously something to do with Mabel Monk, wouldn't you say?

Romney And why should that concern *me*? The bitch has been dead thirty years.

Douglas Have you told the police about these? (*He shakes the cuttings*)

Romney (*scornfully*) That someone's sending me ancient press cuttings? (*He shakes his head*) Oh, no. There's no need to bring the police into this. (*Smiling oddly*) *I* shall discover the person responsible, then make my own arrangements for dealing with them. No-one—but no-one—attempts to frighten Romney Marsh. (*He glares at him*)

Tanya (*looking up*) Just a minute, Rom. I can see why you suspect one of us of having sent those things to you. We all—at one time or other—had the misfortune to come into contact with darling Mabel. But why would *we* want to do anything like this? None of us could stand her. It wouldn't make sense.

Edith (*nodding*) She's right.

Tanya However—I do have an idea who *may* have sent them.

Everyone stares at her

Romney (*with disbelief*) Really?

Tanya Oh, it's possible I could be *wrong*—though I very much doubt it. But just for the minute let's say it's someone who may blame you for the way she killed herself, and is trying to get back at you.

Romney (*scornfully*) After thirty years? Don't be ridiculous. And how can I be responsible for some over-sexed tart driving her car over a cliff eight thousand miles from here?

Tanya (*soothingly*) I didn't say you were, darling, but there *were* mutterings at the time that *you* caused her breakdown at Stratford.

Edith (*defensively*) Lies. Every one of them. It had nothing to do with Rom.

The woman was incapable of giving a credible performance. Every critic in the country slated her Portia.

Tanya You don't have to convince *me*, Edith. As far as I was concerned, the only performances *that* little cow could manage, were the ones that took place in her bedrooms. But the person I'm thinking of, could believe otherwise and have some idiotic thought of revenge in mind. (*After a momentary hesitation*) Did any of you know she was English?

There is a surprised reaction

Douglas English? But her parents were American. Hollywood film extras. Everyone knows that.

Tanya (*shaking her head*) I got to know her quite well during the time we were making *Hallo, Baby*. She told me herself she was actually born here and taken to America when her real parents separated. The woman everyone assumed was her mother, was in fact her father's common-law wife, a divorcee with a two-year-old daughter of her own. The two of them were brought up as sisters.

Romney (*acidly*) I assume there's some point to all this?

Tanya (*pressing on*) When she came over here in fifty-nine to make the film, her *real* mother crawled out of the woodwork. I used to see her now and again, hanging around outside the studios, waiting for Mabel to finish, but of course, I'd no idea who she was at that time. I just assumed she was a fan. But one night Mabel introduced us. There was also a younger sister she never knew she had. I met them a couple more times before we finished the film and got the full story.

Edith If what you're saying's true, why hasn't it come out before? The muck-rakers have dragged up almost everything she did from the cradle to the grave, during the past thirty years, and no-one's even *hinted* at anything like this.

Tanya (*drily*) Of course they haven't. And there's a very good reason. Her so-called parents separated when she was seventeen, and the stepmother left Hollywood to go back East, taking her own daughter with her. She died there in nineteen fifty-one and no-one knows what happened to the girl. Arthur Monk, her father, died of cancer sometime in fifty-four ... which meant, of course, there was no way anyone could discover the truth from *him*, either.

Edith But what about her birth certificate? That would have shown who her real parents were, surely?

Tanya Of course it would. If they could have found it. But by the time the investigations began, every scrap of information referring to her early life had gone. Presumably destroyed. Monk was only a stage name anyway ... no-one knew what her real name was and for the life of me, I can't remember what the mother and sister called themselves.

Romney (*sarcastically*) Forgive me for being obtuse, but I fail to see what this has to do with those cuttings.

Tanya I've almost finished. As you must remember ... just before she killed herself, she told someone at Fox Studios that her sister had arrived to take care of the baby. From all accounts, the woman never left the grounds and managed to keep pretty much out of sight. In fact, come the great day, she never even went to the *funeral*. While half Hollywood turned out to cheer, *she* vanished into thin air taking Mabel's baby with her. Even today, no-one's any idea of where they went. It's just another Hollywood legend.

She looks from one to the other. They gaze back at her intently

I swore I wouldn't reveal this to a living soul—well—not till I'd published my autobiography—but I'm damned sure *I* know what *actually* happened over there.

Romney (*drily*) We're all agog.

Tanya The sister was her *real* sister . . . not the one everyone *thought* it was. For the last thirty years, *they've been looking for the wrong person*. (*Earnestly*) Don't you see? After meeting up with her real mother and sister when we were making *Hallo, Baby*, she must have invited one or both of them to Hollywood during the time she spent in the clinic. They were actually *there* when the child was born. When she killed herself, they simply took the baby and what jewellery and cash they could lay their hands on, and came back to England.

Douglas So what you're saying is—these cuttings may have been sent to Rom by Mabel's mother, or sister? (*He moves upstage* R, *thoughtfully*)

Edith *Or* baby. (*Smiling*) Isn't that being a little fanciful, Tanya? It all sounds like one of those far-fetched plots dreamed up by the writers of American soap-operas.

Tanya Doesn't it? But if you'll give me a couple of minutes, I think I'll be able to prove it to you. (*She rises*)

Romney What do you mean? Where are you going?

Tanya Hopefully, to have a few words with the sender of those cuttings. (*She moves to the door*)

Edith (*incredulous*) You mean—one of them's *here*? In this house?

Tanya If they aren't, then my eyes are playing tricks. But there's one way to find out, isn't there? Then, perhaps, we can see what this is all about.

Tanya exits L

Romney If she's wasting my time . . .

Douglas (*shaking his head*) No. She's serious. And if she *is* right, we may have stumbled on to something more——(*He breaks off and glances at the door* R)

Edith What is it?

Douglas moves rapidly to the door R, *and opens it to look inside the other room*

What's wrong?

Douglas (*frowning as he closes the door again*) I thought I heard something.

Romney (*suspiciously*) What kind of something?

Douglas (*slightly embarrassed*) I'm not sure. Maybe the other door closing. Room's empty enough now.

Edith (*frowning*) You mean someone could have been in there listening to us?

Douglas (*after momentary thought*) No. I probably imagined it. (*He glances at the door again then dismisses it from mind*) What was I saying?

Lynda enters L

Lynda Oh—am I interrupting anything?
Douglas Well——
Lynda (*quickly*) It's all right. I'll go away again. I just thought you may have finished when I saw Tanya going down the hall. (*To Romney*) Can I be a pest and help myself to a drop of Scotch? It's not that I'm a *total* inebriate, but I simply can't get to sleep at night unless I've had a drink or two. Preferably two. (*She laughs*)
Romney (*not too graciously*) By all means. Help yourself.

Lynda turns to the drinks table and helps herself to a drink

Lynda I just *love* the house. And that *divine* conservatory. (*Looking at him*) I didn't know you went in for exotics, Rom. The perfumes are enough to knock you out.

Harriet appears in the doorway L

Harriet Excuse me, sir. I was looking for Miss Mason. She was asking for Miss Bakewell. (*She turns to leave*)

Edith and Douglas exchange quick looks

Romney (*to Harriet*) Wait. *Did* she say why?
Harriet (*turning back*) No, sir. She just asked if I'd seen her, but I hadn't. Until now, that is. I think I just saw her running up the stairs.
Romney (*suspiciously*) Did you see from which direction she came, Mrs Bales?
Harriet Oh, no sir. It was just a glimpse as I came along the corridor.
Romney I see. Thank you.
Harriet (*hesitantly*) Will that be all for tonight, sir?
Romney Unless anyone cares for hot milk, or suchlike? (*He glances at the others*)

Everyone demurs

Very well. You may retire, Mrs Bales.
Harriet Thank you, sir. Good-night.

Harriet turns and exits

Douglas (*to the others*) Excuse me. Won't be a moment.

He puts the cuttings down on top of the desk and follows her out

Romney (*to Edith*) What do you know about the Bakewell girl?
Edith (*frowning*) Not much. George Kaye recommended her. She'd done rep at Birmingham, Leeds and Liverpool, and a couple of small roles for BBC. She read well, so Douggie gave her the part.
Romney (*crossing to the armchair and sitting*) I want her investigated. Find out exactly who she is and where she came from.

Lynda (*looking from one to the other*) Can *I* be of any help?

Romney (*snapping at her*) Keep out of things that don't concern you. This is a personal matter.

Lynda (*backing off*) Sorry I spoke. But I *do* know her quite well, and if you'd any questions ... (*She turns to leave the room*)

Edith (*standing*) Wait. (*To Romney*) Maybe she *can* help, Rom. (*To Lynda*) How long have you known her?

Lynda (*after a slight pause*) About nine years. I did some designs for *Separate Tables*, and Stella was playing Miss Tanner. We found we'd a lot in common and kept in touch. I've stayed at her parents' place in Derby a couple of times. In fact, last year they asked me up for their Silver Wedding celebrations.

Romney Twenty-five years? But the girl's older than that. Much older.

Lynda Well. (*Hesitantly*) Actually, they aren't her *real* parents. She's a foster-child. Her real mother had a drink problem and couldn't cope with her, so the Bakewells took her in. It was the best thing that ever happened to her. She absolutely adores them.

Bradford enters L, *mopping at his hand with a bloodstained handkerchief*

Bradford (*to Romney*) *Love* all the campery, Rom, but daubing Kensington Gore on the banister rail *does* seem a teensy bit over the top.

Romney (*glaring at him*) What are you talking about?

Bradford (*dangling the stained handkerchief*) This, dear heart. The red sticky stuff. I hope Mrs Thing won't mind rinsing it through for me. It's the only one I've got with me.

Edith Let me see. (*She moves to Brad and takes the handkerchief, examining it gingerly*) This isn't stage blood. It's *real*.

Bradford (*dismayed*) But it's all down the stair-rail. (*He rubs at his hand in distaste*)

Lynda (*hesitantly*) Could someone have had a nosebleed or something?

Romney (*standing; to Edith*) Get the others. I want to see them here at once.

Edith exits L

Bradford (*staring at his hands in distaste*) I'd better go wash my hands.

Romney (*sharply*) No. No-one else leaves this room until I find out what this is all about. (*He turns to the fireplace*) First of all I am *threatened*. Then my intelligence is insulted by stories of revenge for events that happened thirty years ago, and now blood is found smeared all over my house. (*With great emphasis*) I will not have this. *Any* of it. (*He whirls about and glares at them fiercely*) Sit down. Both of you.

Puzzled and uneasy, they sit on the settee

Something is happening here that makes me very angry. Someone—for reasons best known to themselves is trying to play games with me. However, I warn you, I'm an excellent player of games and have made it a rule of my life never to lose. *Never*. (*In softer tones*) They come here to my home. Accept my hospitality and then try to make a fool of me. Frighten

me. Have a good laugh at my expense. But I tell you this—*all of you*—
Romney Marsh will have the last laugh.

Caroline enters L, looking defiant

Caroline Well? (*She glares at Marsh*)
Romney (*indicating a chair*) Sit down.
Caroline (*frostily*) I prefer to stand, thank you.
Romney (*snapping*) This is my house, and you will do as I tell you.
Caroline (*sneering*) And what will you do if I don't? Toss me into the moat,
    or lock me in a dungeon? I presume there *is* a dungeon in this crack-pot
    film set you call a house?
Bradford (*defensively*) Now listen——
Caroline (*turning on him*) And as for *you*, you pathetic excuse for a man. I
    used to respect you as an actor, but I've had my eyes opened today.
    You're nothing more than another spineless sycophant who's so desper-
    ate for work you'd swallow *any* insult in exchange for a bit part. Well just
    wait till I get back to London. I'm going to see this little escapade reaches
    the ears of every gossip columnist in the country.

*Stella enters the room L. She is in dressing-gown and slippers and looks
surprised at seeing everyone*

Stella You wanted to see me, Mr Marsh? (*She glances at Lynda quickly*)
Romney (*snapping*) Come in. (*He indicates the armchair*) Sit there.
Caroline Jump to it, darling. Otherwise he might lock you in the Iron
    Maiden.
Stella Has something happened? (*She moves to the chair and sits*) There's
    blood on the stair-rail.
Caroline Another charming little touch of Mr Marsh's, dear. It goes with
    the shrunken heads for door-handles. (*Sweetly*) If you look closely
    enough, I'm sure you'll find his bookmarks are human tongues—torn out
    at the roots. (*She glares at Marsh*)
Romney (*sharply*) That is *enough*. One more word, and I warn you, you'll
    never work in the West End again—not to mention half the rep
    companies in Britain. And don't make the mistake of thinking I can't do
    it, because you'd be wrong, Miss Clavers. *Very* wrong.

Edith enters L and he falls silent

Edith Freddy will be down in a minute or two. I can't seem to find Tanya.
Romney (*to Stella*) Have *you* seen her?
Stella (*startled*) Not since the read-through.
Romney But she came to your room?
Stella (*surprised*) No. Why should she?
Romney Where did you go when you left here fifteen minutes ago?
Stella (*puzzled*) Upstairs. To learn my lines.
Romney (*sarcastically*) Without a script? (*He jabs his finger at her script
    which lies beside the fireside chair in which she sat earlier*) That *is* yours, I
    believe?
Stella (*hesitantly*) Yes.

Romney Then perhaps you'd care to explain?

Stella (*awkwardly*) After I left here, I was half-way up the stairs when I realized I'd left it behind. I was going to come back for it, but then I . . . (*She falters*)

Romney Yes?

Lynda (*standing*) Oh, for God's sake, Rom. Stop making such a song and dance about it. She was scared stiff of you. She thought if she came back, you'd snap her head off, so she dropped in and borrowed mine.

Romney (*to Stella*) Is this true?

Stella (*embarrassed*) Yes.

Freddy enters. He is wrapped in a dressing-gown, and has slippers on his feet

Freddy I've not kept you, have I? I was in the shower. (*He looks at the others*) Is something wrong. Someone hurt?

Romney (*sharply*) Why should they be?

Freddy (*startled*) Well . . . there's something that looks like blood on the stair-rail. I almost put my hand in it.

Romney Have you seen Tanya?

Freddy (*nodding*) A few minutes ago. Yes. She was looking for Stella. But she wasn't in her room, so she came across to see if she was with me.

Lynda (*puzzled*) Why should she do that?

Freddy She thought we might be running over Zoe's lines together. But of course, we weren't. I mean—I was just about to step into the shower.

Bradford Did you see where she was going when she left you?

Freddy (*awkwardly*) Well—no. I only had a towel wrapped round me. (*He glances around*) She's not *missing*, is she? I mean—she can't be far away.

Romney (*to Edith*) Did you check the library?

Edith I—assumed she'd be upstairs.

Romney (*snapping*) Do it now.

Edith (*hesitantly*) Shall I check the rooms at *this* end of the house first?

Romney Do what you like. Just find her.

Edith exits through the door R

Stella (*concerned*) You don't think something's happened to her, do you?

Freddy (*puzzled*) Why should it have? She was fine a few minutes ago.

Lynda But where did the blood come from? And how did it get on to the stair-rail?

Edith enters R, looking shaken

Everyone stares at her as she stumbles blindly towards Romney

Edith (*fighting for control*) Tanya—she's dead.

There is a general reaction

She's lying in there with her *throat* cut.

Everyone looks at the door R

Romney pushes Edith aside, moves over to the door and exits

Lynda But . . . but she *can't* be. There's only us in the house.

Edith collapses on to the settee

Stella (*protesting*) There must be some mistake.
Caroline (*drily*) Bet your life there's some mistake. Tanya Mason's as dead as I am. (*Laughing harshly*) This is something they've cooked up between them. A little entertainment for the weekend. Any moment now, she's going to come swanning through that door, shouting "Fooled you, darlings" and laughing her silly head off because you fell for it.

Romney enters R, *looking dazed. He moves slowly into the room and nods in disbelief*

Freddy (*nervously*) Hadn't someone better call the police?
Romney (*looking at him in amazement*) Are you mad? We can't have the police here.
Edith (*protesting*) But if she's been killed, we *have* to call them.
Romney Impossible. Think of the publicity.
Lynda (*stunned*) But we've got to do *something*.
Caroline Yes. And I'm going to do it right now. (*She crosses to the door* R *and opens it*) All right, darling.

She exits into the room

(*Off*) You've had your bit of fun and we're all suitably impressed, so can we stop playing games and——(*She screams loudly*)

A moment later, she comes hurrying out, looking shaken

Oh, my God. (*She totters* CB)
Romney (*bitterly*) Satisfied, Miss Clavers?
Caroline (*staring at him*) *You* did it, didn't you? You're the one who killed her. You're mad. Stark, staring mad. I knew it from the minute I set eyes on you.
Edith (*gamely*) Don't be ridiculous. He couldn't *possibly* have done it. He hasn't moved from here since she left the room.

Douglas hurries into the room, L

Caroline (*wildly*) I don't care. *He* killed her. *Him.*
Douglas Killed who? What's happened? (*He looks from one to the other*)
Bradford (*without a trace of effeminacy*) It's Tanya. She's been murdered.
Douglas (*incredulous*) What?
Bradford Through there. (*He indicates the door* R) Edith's just found her.

Douglas stares at him then hurries off R

Stella (*standing*) Excuse me. I don't feel very well.
Romney (*sharply*) No. Nobody leaves this room.
Stella (*faintly*) I'm sorry. (*She lurches blindly towards the door* L)
Romney (*calling angrily*) Come back.

Stella exits hurriedly

Caroline glares at Marsh, then follows her off

Edith It's all right, Rom. (*She goes to him*) Let them go. We have to talk.

Romney (*harshly*) Talk? What good will talk do? (*He shrugs her hand off*) Don't you understand what this means? A murder's been committed in *my* house. The house of Romney Marsh. I could be *finished*.

Douglas enters the room, looking dazed. He moves to the drinks table and pours himself a generous drink, gulping it down

Edith (*earnestly*) But it's nothing to do with you, Rom. *You* didn't kill her. They can't hold you responsible for *this*. You have two independent witnesses who'll swear you never left the room.

Bradford That's all very well, heart, but where does it leave the rest of us?

Edith (*coldly*) I'm afraid that's *your* problem, Brad. All *I* know is, whoever it was that killed Tanya, Rom, and myself are totally in the clear.

Freddy (*protesting*) But why should any of *us* want to kill her? I've never met her before in my life.

Lynda And *we've* been friends for *years*.

Bradford Same here.

Edith That may be so, but the fact remains, the two of us are the only ones who couldn't possibly have done it.

Freddy sinks dazedly into the easy chair

Douglas (*with an effort*) Has anyone called the police?

Edith (*shaking her head*) Rom thought we should give ourselves time to think.

Douglas I'll do it now. The sooner we get them here, the better. (*He turns towards the door* L)

Romney No. Wait. Wait.

Douglas halts and looks at him

Don't you see? This is something to do with those newspaper cuttings. It's all tied in with *them*. It *has* to be.

Freddy (*blankly*) Newspaper cuttings?

Bradford (*to Romney*) What newspaper cuttings?

Edith (*matter of factly*) The ones he's been receiving since last Monday morning. Contemporary accounts of Mabel Monk's suicide.

Freddy (*puzzled*) But why? I mean—that was back in the sixties, wasn't it?

Lynda And why should they have anything to do with Tanya's murder?

Romney (*deliberately*) Because, my dear Lynda, she thought she knew who'd been sending them. Someone here. In this house. One of *you*.

Bradford (*reverting to high camp*) Well—I've sent a *lot* of things through the post in the last week, sweetie, but I don't seem to recall sending any newspaper cuttings.

Romney No-one's accusing *you*, Brad. But without excessive brain strain, I think we can easily deduce which one of you *did*. (*He smiles nastily*) The person who sent those cuttings was Mabel Monk's illegitimate daughter—the oh, so innocent looking Miss Stella Bakewell.

There is a general reaction

Lynda (*in astonishment*) What?

Romney (*smirking*) Just before Tanya was murdered, she told us she believed Mabel Monk's missing child had been brought back to this country and raised by its aunt as her own.

Freddy absently selects a chocolate from the box beside him and pops it into his mouth, his eyes still riveted on Romney

She also believed that grown-up child was here — in this house, and left the room fully intending to return with her *plus* an explanation for those cuttings. Both Mrs Bales and Mr Bostock have told us Tanya was looking for Miss Bakewell. It therefore follows Miss Bakewell is the daughter of Mabel Monk, and Tanya Mason's murderer.

Lynda (*protesting*) But that's ridiculous. Stella's mother was a dipsomaniac ... not a Hollywood film star. And even if she *had* been Mabel's daughter, why should she kill Tanya just to prevent her telling anyone?

Freddy selects another chocolate

Besides — it's impossible for her to have done it. According to Mrs Bales, Tanya had just asked her if she'd seen Stella and been told no. A few moments later, according to Freddy, Tanya was upstairs looking for Stella. Isn't that right, Freddy?

Everyone looks at Freddy, who is about to put the chocolate in his mouth. He looks at it in surprise, then quickly returns it to the box

Freddy Er — yes. Yes. She came to my room as I told you.

Douglas And Mrs Bales came looking for her *here* to say she thought she'd just seen Stella hurrying upstairs.

Romney If there's a point to this rigmarole, Douglas, kindly make it. You're telling us nothing we don't already know.

Douglas Well isn't it obvious? Stella couldn't possibly have had time to kill Tanya *upstairs*, carry her *downstairs* and put her next door, then get back *upstairs* to her room again before Edith arrived to tell her you wanted to see her.

Lynda And don't forget. She also came to *my* room to borrow my script.

Edith (*coldly*) So she killed her *before* she went upstairs.

Douglas No. If you remember, just before Lynda came in, I looked into the next room. It was empty. And at that time, *Tanya was still upstairs.* Freddy was speaking to her.

Bradford Then ... ?

Douglas Whoever killed Tanya, had to be waiting for her down here. On this floor.

Romney and Edith look at Lynda as ...

Caroline enters, L

Caroline (*acidly*) Would it come as a great surprise if I told you the telephone is out of order?

Douglas (*turning to her*) What?

Caroline (*heavily*) I tried to call nine-nine-nine, but the line's completely dead. I couldn't get a sound out of it.

Freddy (*standing*) Would you like *me* to try? (*He moves towards the door* L) I know a *bit* about them. Perhaps it's just a loose connection?

Caroline Be my guest. But while you're wasting your time, I'm climbing into my car and heading for the nearest town, fog or no fog. I'm not spending another minute under this madman's roof, and that's flat.

Romney I'm afraid your departure will be quite out of the question, Miss Clavers. Like it or not, until Monday morning, you're a guest in my house, and there's nothing either of us can do about it.

Caroline Is that so? Well just watch me. (*She turns to exit*)

Romney (*raising his voice slightly*) In that case, I hope you're fond of dogs, Miss Clavers. Because there're eighteen of them roaming the grounds at the present time, just waiting to sink their teeth into anyone foolish enough to venture outside.

Bradford (*shocked*) Not those bloody Dobermanns I saw out back?

Caroline turns and stares at Romney

Romney I'm afraid so. (*He smiles wryly*) I released them from their kennels just before dinner. Naturally I was not expecting anyone to be *murdered* here this weekend, but it *was* my intention to prevent anyone leaving before I'd settled the little matter of those mysterious cuttings. I followed the example of Dr Vincent in my film *Hounds of Hell*, and arranged for the security people to deliver the animals yesterday. (*He moves to the easy chair and sits*) However, although it seems my original suspicions were unfounded, the dogs will still serve their purpose. No-one can possibly leave "Usher" until their handlers arrive on Monday morning. Should anyone set foot outside the house, there's every possibility it's the last thing they'll *ever* do.

Caroline I told you he was mad. *Now* will you believe me?

Lynda (*dismayed*) But we can't spend all weekend trapped inside the house. Not with a murderer on the loose.

Romney (*flatly*) We have no other choice.

Freddy (*quickly*) I'd better have a look at that phone. Maybe I can fix it.

He exits L, *followed by Caroline*

Douglas (*shaking his head*) I don't believe this is actually happening. It's like a situation from one of those damned horror films you've been appearing in for the past twenty-five years. Thick fog, savage dogs roaming the grounds, telephone out of order, a dead body in the next room. It's got to be just some sort of bizarre practical joke.

Bradford Some joke, sweetie. With Tanya's throat slit from ear to ear.

Lynda (*wincing*) Don't.

Edith (*suddenly*) That girl. *Caroline.*

Douglas What about her?

Edith If Stella couldn't have killed Tanya, it has to be *her*. She must have been listening in the next room while we were talking. Remember? You thought you heard someone. When Tanya left here, she must have met her in the hall, killed her, left her body through there, then hurried back to her room. I thought she looked flushed when I went to fetch her, but assumed she'd been crying.

Lynda But if Caroline's Mabel Monk's daughter, why should she kill *Tanya*? I mean—Tanya obviously thought *Stella* was the person she wanted, or why would she go looking for her?

Edith Quite. But Tanya didn't mention any names. What she *said* was she thought she knew the identity of Mabel's child. Caroline simply *assumed* she'd been recognized and killed her to keep her quiet.

Bradford I'm sure you're right, darling. You always are. But I'm still a teensy bit confused as to the *reason* for all this. Why commit murder just to conceal the fact you've been sending press cuttings through the post? It's not exactly the *strongest* motive I've ever heard.

Douglas (*quietly*) Unless, of course, she intended something similar for Rom.

Romney (*incredulous*) Because I rejected her mother thirty years ago? Don't be ridiculous.

Edith Rejected? (*Puzzled*) What do you mean?

Romney Exactly what I said. We were going to be married. I terminated the relationship during rehearsals at Stratford.

Everyone looks at him in astonishment

We met in London when she was filming *Hallo, Baby*, and I was completing *The Case of Dr Strange*. Preferring to keep our interest in each other a closely guarded secret, we agreed to make no announcement until after the Stratford season. It was a wise decision under the circumstances. During the rehearsal period, I discovered she was expecting another man's child. I was left with no option but to withdraw my offer of marriage.

Douglas stares at him

Bradford So *that's* what happened? *That's* why she went to pieces and couldn't learn the part? But how come nobody *knew*?

Romney (*flatly*) I am not in the habit of discussing my personal life with others, as well you know, and had this present situation not arisen, the story would have gone to my grave with me. (*He selects a chocolate from the box beside him*)

Edith (*bitterly*) Why couldn't you have told *me*?

Romney For the simple reason that even those most loyal can let things slip in unguarded moments. Reveal things they are not supposed to know and——(*He stops suddenly and gazes blindly into space*)

Lynda (*curiously*) What is it?

Romney (*softly*) What a fool I've been. What a blind, unthinking idiot. We were wrong. *All* wrong. We were looking at the wrong person. (*With growing realization*) She didn't know, did she? How could she have done? She wasn't even here. (*He puts the chocolate in his mouth*)

Lynda Who wasn't?

Romney Tanya, of course. She wasn't here when we——(*He chokes and clutches at his throat*) Ahhh. Ahhhhhhhh.

Edith (*startled*) Quick. He's choking.

Romney (*struggling for air*) Lying . . . Lying . . . (*He collapses to the floor in a heap, limbs twitching feebly*)

Bradford (*flinging himself beside Romney*) Rom. Rom. (*He attempts to revive him*)

Lynda (*urgently*) Loosen his collar. (*She kneels beside them to help*)

Bradford (*attempting to do it then stopping*) Too late. He's dead.

Edith (*stricken*) Oh, my God. Oh, my God.

They all stare at Romney's body as—

—the CURTAIN *falls*

ACT II

Scene 1

The same. Early Sunday morning

Apart from the removal of Marsh's body and the envelope of clippings, everything is as it was. The drapes are still drawn and the room silent and almost dark. Both doors are closed

After a moment, the door L opens, and a weary looking Harriet enters, a screwed-up handkerchief clutched in her fist. She moves up to the windows and opens the drapes. Dull grey light filters in. Turning front, she surveys the room, finally allowing her eyes to rest on the spot where Romney died. Dabbing at her eyes, she takes a deep breath and turns to exit. As she does so . . .

Stella enters L

Both react in shock

Stella (*recovering*) I'm sorry. I didn't realize there was anyone else about.

Harriet (*flustered and hiding the handkerchief*) That's all right, miss. I was just opening the drapes.

Stella I—couldn't sleep. I was trying not to make a noise and wake the others.

Harriet (*nodding*) I've hardly slept myself. In the end I thought I may as well come down and make an early start with the breakfasts. Or at least do something to keep my mind off—what happened here last night. I still can't really believe it. (*Remembering her position*) Would you like a coffee or something, miss? It wouldn't take a minute.

Stella (*wearily*) Perhaps a bit later. To be honest, I don't know what I *do* want . . . except to wake up from this awful nightmare. (*She sits on settee*)

Harriet (*kindly*) Well, if you *do* change your mind you've only to ask. (*She turns to go*)

Stella (*suddenly*) Mrs Bales?

Harriet (*turning again*) Yes, miss?

Stella Last night. When you saw Miss Mason. Are you *quite* sure she didn't say why she was looking for me?

Harriet (*nodding*) Yes, miss. She just wanted to know where you were. (*Her face crumples*) Oh, that poor woman. If only she hadn't come here, she'd still be alive. (*She brushes at her eyes*)

Stella (*quietly*) Yes. (*She suddenly frowns*) Did *you* know Mr Marsh had a weak heart?

Harriet (*shaking her head*) I'd no idea, miss. He'd always appeared very healthy for a man his age . . . though he did have his "off-days" of course, like most of us.

Stella (*curiously*) How long had you worked for him?

Harriet Almost a year, miss. Since his previous housekeeper retired. I heard she was leaving, you see, and applied for the job. Being on my own, living in the country didn't bother me, but I don't know what I'll do now. Jobs aren't so easy come by at my age.

Stella No. I suppose not. (*Suddenly*) Had you met any of the *present* guests prior to last night?

Harriet Well—Miss Cartwright, of course. But I don't recall any of the others. Mr Marsh wasn't a very *social* person, you understand.

Stella (*thoughtfully*) No. No. Of course not. (*She smiles*) Thank you.

Harriet (*at a loss*) Well . . . I'll get back to the breakfasts, then.

She gives a puzzled look at Stella, then exits L

Wearily, Stella massages her temples, then glances at the door R. *Standing, she hesitantly approaches it and comes to a halt, her hand outstretched to grasp the knob*

Bradford Kyle enters sleepily behind her, dressing-gown over his pyjamas, and wearing slippers

Bradford (*yawning*) Ah. It was *you*, was it?

Stella turns quickly to face him

I thought I heard someone tippy-toeing past my door a few minutes ago. Had a rough night, eh?

Stella (*nodding*) Horrible. (*She moves to the settee again*)

Bradford Can't say it's the best one *I've* ever spent, either. (*He moves to the window and peers out*) Still thick out there. Not much chance of the local fuzz paying a surprise visit *today*, by the look of it.

Stella (*sitting*) No. I suppose not.

Bradford (*moving to the fireplace*) Be thankful for small mercies, eh? Gives us a few more hours of calm before the storm breaks.

Stella (*looking at him in a puzzled manner*) Storm?

Bradford You don't imagine *this* little episode's going to slip past without attracting media attention, do you? It was bad enough when Tanya managed to get her throat cut, but when they find out *Romney Marsh* had a fatal heart attack on the same night *and* in the next room, they'll be down on us like a pack of wolves. Most of us will be lucky if we ever work again.

Stella What do you mean? Why shouldn't we?

Bradford Let's face it, sweetie. No matter how much we'd like to put it out of our minds, one of our merry little band was responsible for Tanya's tracheotomy, and unless there's a Hercule Poirot or Sherlock Holmes attached to the CID these days, I can't see any possibility of them discovering which of us it was. From a managerial point of view, it's not a very satisfactory arrangement, is it? Would *you* employ Thespians with possible murderous tendencies? I think not. We're going to be under suspicion for the rest of our lives.

Stella (*protesting*) But that's idiotic. *I* didn't kill her.

Bradford Neither did I, heart. But how do we *prove* it?

There is a short silence

Stella (*hesitantly*) We could try to find something out ourselves. Before the police arrive.

Bradford (*amused*) Play detectives, you mean?

Stella Why not? It's better than just sitting around waiting to be rescued.

Bradford (*shrugging*) All right. But I warn you. I'm not very good at it. (*Grinning*) What do we do first? Grill the suspects? (*He sits on the settee arm*)

Stella (*bashfully*) As a matter of fact, I've already made a start. I've been making a mental list of those who couldn't possibly have killed her. (*She ticks them on her fingers*) Edith ... Mr Marsh ... Lynda—

Bradford (*breaking in*) What makes you think *she* couldn't have done it?

Stella (*surprised*) Lynda? Well ... because—she *couldn't* have. I mean—I've known her for years. She couldn't kill *anybody*. And besides ... she and Tanya were friends.

Bradford Tanya and *I* were friends, but there were times I could have murdered her myself. (*Seriously*) She wasn't an angel, you know. If anyone crossed her, she'd stop at nothing to get even. (*Rising*) That woman was so devious, she could stab you in the back and you wouldn't know you were dead till twenty years later. (*He moves to the fireplace*) There's one poor zombie upstairs who *still* doesn't know it, and——(*He stops dead in his tracks, a startled look on his face*)

Stella (*staring at him*) What? What is it?

Bradford (*blinking and recovering himself*) Oh. Nothing. I—er—was just thinking out loud, that's all. (*Flashing a broad smile*) Is that coffee I can smell? Just what I need to save my life. I—er—I'll see you later, eh? We'll talk about it some more.

He begins to exit L, *and almost collides with* ...

A tired-looking Lynda as she enters. She wears a skirt and blouse, but has no make-up on and her hair has been hastily brushed

Sorry.

Bradford vanishes into the hall

Lynda gazes after him, then turns her head to see Stella

Lynda (*wearily*) Thank God it's morning. (*She crosses behind the settee to* R) I've had the most *awful* night. You wouldn't believe the dreams. Nothing but blood and dead bodies and people chasing each other up and down corridors with knives in their hands. (*She slumps into the easy chair*)

Stella Would you like some tea? I can ask Mrs Bales to make you some. (*She rises*)

Lynda (*shaking her head*) I couldn't face it at this hour. It's not six o'clock yet. I haven't been up this early in years.

Stella Do you feel like talking? There's something I'd like to discuss. About last night.

Lynda (*frowning*) What about it?

Stella (*hesitating*) I've been thinking things over. (*Moving closer to Lynda*) About what happened. It doesn't add up. There's something wrong.

Lynda (*puzzled*) In what way?

Stella (*throwing a glance at the door* L) I don't think Mr Marsh had a heart attack at all. I think he was murdered.

Lynda (*startled*) What?

Stella That chocolate. The one you all thought he'd choked on. It was poisoned. I'm sure of it.

Lynda (*disbelievingly*) Of course it wasn't poisoned. He had a heart attack. We all agreed.

Stella I don't care what you *agreed*. Someone in this house *poisoned* him. And that someone was the same person who cut Tanya Mason's throat.

Lynda (*shaking her head*) But that's ridiculous. If anyone *had* wanted to kill Rom, they'd have come up with something more certain than a poisoned *chocolate*. How could they be sure *he'd* eat it? He could have offered them to someone else. Then what? The wrong person would have died. No. It was a heart attack. It had to be.

Stella (*doggedly*) But there was nothing wrong with his heart. I asked Mrs Bales a few minutes ago.

Lynda (*patiently*) How would *she* know? She's only been with him a few months. Edith's been worried about him for *years*. She said so. The trouble was, he wouldn't have anything to do with doctors. He preferred to dose himself up with herbs and things.

Stella (*heatedly*) I don't care if he chewed rabbit droppings. In my opinion he suddenly realized who the murderer was, but already had the chocolate in his mouth. He was trying to tell you just before he started choking. Don't your remember? He said he'd been looking at the wrong person for Tanya's killer?

Lynda Well ... yes. He'd been looking at *you*, hadn't he? He thought *you* were Mabel's daughter because Tanya had gone looking for you. But we all know *now* it was only because she'd seen you wearing that outfit I'd designed and the resemblance had been so extraordinary. I could hardly believe you weren't Mabel, myself.

Stella (*determinedly*) All right. But you do agree he'd suddenly realized who the *real* murderer was ... poisoned chocolate or no poisoned chocolate?

Lynda (*tiredly*) I don't know, Stella. I really don't. People say things ... He was choking.

Stella But *not at that moment*. You said so yourself.

Douglas enters the room. He is dressed

He said "Tanya wasn't here when ..." and *then* he started to choke. So what was he *going* to say? She wasn't here when *what*? And who did he mean was lying?

Douglas (*heavily*) That's something we're never going to know unless the police can manage to make sense of it all. I still can't take it in. One of *us* has actually committed murder ... and probably brought on Rom's heart attack in the bargain. (*Sitting on the settee*) It's too incredible for words. It's the end for all of us. You do realize that, don't you?

Stella That's just what Brad said a few minutes ago. And it's why we've got to *do* something before they arrive.

Lynda (*wearily*) So what do you suggest? We ask whoever it was to confess and let the rest of us off the hook?

Stella Of course not. But we've got two options. Firstly, we try to find out who the *real* murderer is, or secondly, if everybody agrees to it, we provide the police with a solution that will keep them happy.

Douglas And how do we do that?

Stella (*flatly*) We tell the police that Rom killed her.

They look at her in astonishment

Douglas You're—not *serious*, are you?

Lynda You can't accuse an innocent man of murder—even if he *is* dead.

Douglas And what about the *real* murderer? We'd be giving him the opportunity to walk away scot-free.

Stella Which is more than *we'll* ever do if the police never find out who it is.

Douglas (*shaking his head*) I'm sorry. It's totally out of the question. And I think the rest of them will back me up on that.

Stella (*sighing*) Then that's that, isn't it? We'll just have to keep our fingers crossed. (*She moves behind the settee*) But all the same, I'm not going to sit around for the next twenty-four hours and do nothing. Like it or not, I'm going to try and get to the bottom of this.

Stella exits L

Lynda (*standing*) She's convinced herself that Rom was murdered too. With a poisoned chocolate. I *told* her she was wrong but she won't listen. Do you think I should try again?

Douglas (*nodding*) It might be an idea. We've got to last out till tomorrow morning and the less we rock the boat, the better. If she asks the wrong person the wrong questions—well—they've already killed once.

Lynda (*concerned*) I'll do it now.

Lynda hurries from the room

Douglas stands and rubs his forehead, then moves up to the window R, and gazes out

Douglas Damn. Damn. Damn.

Bradford enters L, carrying a mug of coffee

Bradford Something wrong?

Douglas (*turning*) Who pulled the stake out of *your* heart? It's not seven o'clock yet. (*He moves down to the fireplace*)

Bradford I've just been up to your room. Wanted to have a quiet word with you. Alone. (*He closes the door behind him and moves to the settee*)

Douglas Oh?

Bradford It's been some years since we had a *private* little get-together, hasn't it, Douggie? Over thirty of them, come to think of it. (*He sits*)

Douglas (*frowning*) And what's *that* supposed to mean?

Bradford Don't say you've *forgotten*. (*Archly*) That divine little flat in Windsor? Your twenty-third birthday party? All that lovely wine?

Douglas (*warningly*) Brad . . .

Bradford (*raising a hand*) Oh, don't worry. I've not had a sudden urge to recreate the past. Your secret's safe with me.

Douglas (*tightly*) What "secret"? Nothing happened.

Bradford (*in mock surprise*) Didn't it? (*He sips at his coffee*)

Douglas No, it didn't. And you damn well know it. I was stoned out of my mind.

Bradford (*sadly*) That's true, heart. Dead to the world. But there *were* those rather candid photographs, weren't there? And the camera doesn't lie.

Douglas (*harshly*) Doesn't it? It's fooled the public into accepting *you* as a man for the last twenty-nine years.

Bradford (*carefully*) If I were a vindictive old queen—which I'm not—I could feel very hurt at that statement, Douggie. As a matter of fact, I'm deeply ashamed of what happened that night. You didn't deserve it and I'm sorry . . . though I don't expect you to believe it.

Douglas (*bitterly*) Is that supposed to make me feel better? Do you think that makes up for what I went through afterwards? I almost *killed* myself. If it hadn't been for Tanya, I probably *would* have done.

Bradford (*oddly*) Ah, yes. Sweet darling Tanya. Always there with a shoulder to cry on. She was very good to *me*, too. Got me my first job in show business. Did she ever tell you that?

Douglas (*glancing sharply at him*) Why should she? She knew how I felt about you. I could have killed you as soon as look at you.

Bradford (*suddenly*) Was it you who killed *her*?

Douglas (*giving a short harsh laugh*) Don't be *stupid*. Why would *I* want to kill her?

Bradford (*shrugging*) Maybe because you'd found out that *she* was the one who'd arranged to have those photographs taken.

Douglas (*staring at him in disbelief*) What?

Bradford (*nodding*) I was seventeen at the time and desperate to get my Equity card. There was a showbiz party at the *Ivy* one night and I managed to gate-crash. That's where I first met Tanya. She wasn't a star then, of course, but she was working at it. As a matter of fact, she was in the middle of shooting *Hallo, Baby* with the delectable Mabel Monk. (*He pauses*) Do you see where I'm leading?

Douglas (*tightly*) Go on.

Bradford (*standing*) Tanya wasn't happy. In fact she was downright miserable. She had this problem, you see. She'd fallen for a young clerk in the Studio accounts office—one Douglas Dekker, Esq.—and just as she thought she'd landed him, the aforementioned Miss Monk swooped down like a hawk and carried him off in her dainty little claws.

Douglas (*harshly*) That's ridiculous. There was nothing between Tanya and me at that time. We were just good friends.

Bradford (*shrugging*) Not according to Tanya. Naturally, she wasn't going to just sit back and let her get away with it. Which is where *I* came in. She arranged that dinner party for your birthday, as you know, and made

sure I got a personal invitation to attend. Mabel wasn't there, of course
... they were doing some night shooting ... but she was coming along
later. Tanya slipped something into your drink, and when you passed out,
arranged for a taxi to take you, me and the photographer back to your
flat in Windsor for the photo session. The prints were delivered anony-
mously to Mabel's dressing-room the following afternoon during filming
and Tanya got me my Equity card as a reward.

Douglas (*stunned*) My God.

Bradford It was a job, Douggie. My entrance fee to the world of high living.
If it'll make you feel better, I never actually touched you—except for the
benefit of the photos. But you'd no way of knowing that, had you? All
you *did* know was that you'd been in bed with *me*, Mabel had seen the
pictures of us and flatly refused to see or speak to you again during the
remainder of her stay in England. It all went exactly as planned.

Douglas (*in a whisper*) We were going to be married. I'd bought the ring that
very morning.

Bradford (*after a moment*) I suppose it was yours, was it? The baby she was
expecting when she went to Stratford?

Douglas (*dully*) I don't know. It might have been. I didn't know about it till
... till just before she died. We'd only slept together the once. It could
have been anyone's. Someone she'd met later. On the re-bound. I thought
maybe I'd *driven* her to it. Then last night—when—when he said—(*He
breaks off*)

Bradford That he'd broken their engagement after finding she was pregnant?

Douglas (*nodding*) That's when I realized he'd done *his* share to destroy her,
too. I'd never blamed him before, you see. He was almost impossible with
all actresses. I'd always felt *I* was responsible for what happened at
Stratford. That it was because of *us* she'd had her breakdown. But when
he said that, everything turned upside down. I can't tell you what I felt. I
wasn't even listening to what else was being said. I don't remember
anything until he started choking and had his heart attack. For the first
time since she died, I felt a weight lifting off me. But now this. *Tanya* (*He
sits in the armchair*)

Bradford She was a determined lady. But you never *did* marry her, did you?

Douglas (*turning to him*) We were engaged for a while, but things fizzled out
between us when she went off to Hollywood to do a film for Columbia.
That's where she met her first and second husbands. When she finally
came back to England, everything had changed. She was a star and I was
just another small agent. She took shares and brought a lot of new names
on to the books. Lifted me into the major league and allowed me to move
into management. I owed her a lot. Looked on her as a friend. (*He gives a
hollow laugh*) Friend. If I'd known what you've just told me, I'd have cut
her throat myself.

Bradford That's what I figured. But if you didn't do it, then I'm back to
square one. (*He grins wryly*) I always knew I'd make a rotten detective.

Douglas (*curiously*) What would you have done if you'd been right? Try to
blackmail me?

Bradford (*shrugging*) I might have done. I'm desperately short of cash. That's why I wanted this job so badly. But now that's out of the window …

The doors L open and Edith, in dressing-gown and nightclothes, hurries into the room looking agitated

Edith (*anxiously*) Rom. Where's Rom? What's happened to him?

They stare at her

Where is he?

Douglas (*cautiously*) Upstairs. In his room. We took him there last night. Remember?

Edith (*sharply*) I'm not an idiot. I *know* you did. But he's not there *now*. The room's empty.

Bradford and Douglas exchanges glances

Douglas We'd better take a look.
Edith There's no need. I've *told* you. He's not there.
Bradford (*standing*) I'll check it out.

Bradford exits L

Edith I thought you'd moved him. That there was some reason you'd decided not to leave him there.
Douglas I've not been near the place since we laid him out last night. This is ridiculous. What possible reason could anyone have for moving a corpse? (*Frowning*) Unless Stella's right.
Edith About what?
Douglas She thinks Rom was murdered too.
Edith (*sharply*) Of course he wasn't. How could he have been?
Douglas Poison in one of his chocolates?
Edith She's out of her mind. I told you last night. He'd been having chest pains for months. I wanted him to see a doctor, but you know what he was like. He was afraid they'd diagnose cancer or some other fatal disease. That's why he agreed to do the tour. He thought if he immersed himself in work, he'd be able to ignore it all. (*She sits on the settee*) But the strain was telling on him. His temper grew worse than ever. Last week — when those clippings started arriving — he became almost impossible. At the time I'd no idea *why*, of course, and he flatly refused to answer questions. Then suddenly he insisted on inviting everyone down for the weekend — and the day after, those horrible dogs arrived. That's when I began to get really worried. I couldn't work out what was happening. Everything was so out of character. I realize now what a strain he was under. Tanya's murder was the final straw. His heart couldn't take any more.
Douglas (*deep in thought*) No.
Edith (*bitterly*) If only we could get away from here. Manage to contact the police. (*She looks up suddenly*) Do you think one of us could make it to the

cars? Mine's just round the side of the house. It wouldn't take many minutes to drive to the village and get help.

Douglas (*shaking his head absently*) If it wasn't for this damned fog, it might be worth taking a chance. But those Dobermanns . . . they could tear you to pieces before you'd reached the bottom step. And even if you *did* get to the car, there's still the gates. No. We're better off waiting for someone to come to us.

Edith (*standing*) But we've got to do *something*.

Douglas We shall.

Bradford enters R, *looking worried*

And the first thing to do is find out what's happened to Rom's body.

Bradford I hate to add to our problems, but you'd better make that *two* bodies. Tanya's missing, too.

They look at him in surprise

There's nothing left in there but a patch of dried blood.

Douglas (*quietly*) We'd better get the others. (*To Bradford*) Tell them I want them here now. It's a matter of great urgency.

Brad nods and quickly exits L.

(*Heavily*) Well . . . that's settled the question regarding Rom's death, hasn't it? (*He moves down* R) There's only one reason anyone would want to move his body, and that's to prevent it from being examined.

Edith (*stunned*) But . . . but that means you think he *was* murdered?

Douglas (*nodding*) Yes. Though without a post-mortem, it'll be impossible to prove. And with no body to hand . . . (*He shakes his head*)

Edith (*firmly*) I'm sorry, Douggie. I can't accept that. If anyone *had* wanted to harm Rom, why would they do it here where suspicion would fall on a small group of people, instead of waiting until the tour was under way and widening the possibilities?

Douglas To begin with . . . It's *my* guess that whoever sent those cuttings to Rom expected him to be alone here. If you remember, they started arriving last Monday, but this little gathering of ours wasn't arranged until Thursday afternoon. It's logical to assume the murderer hoped to kill him and be miles away with an airtight alibi before anyone discovered the body. And if it hadn't been for this fog and Rom's idiotic stunt with the dogs, he or she might possibly have got away with it.

Edith (*unconvinced*) But that would mean whoever it was expected to be here anyway, and none of *us* anticipated spending a weekend in the country. It was an invitation out of the blue.

Douglas I know. Which leads me to think Rom had *already* invited someone down here before he asked the rest of us. The question is . . . which one of us was it?

Edith It wasn't *any* of us. The shock of Tanya's murder killed him. Not some supposedly poisoned chocolate.

Douglas Then why was his body moved? And what's happened to Tanya? I'm sorry, Edith. There's no other conclusion I can come to. But right or wrong, we've got to locate them both before the police arrive. For all our sakes.

Edith (*tightly*) I can't see that presenting any problem. They've got to be here in the house, haven't they? Because no-one could get them out. Those terrible dogs would see to that. They were snarling and slavering under my window last night for almost half an hour.

Douglas I know. I heard them myself. (*He glances at the windows*) They seem to have quietened down now, though. Maybe they've gone back to their cages?

Edith Maybe. But I wouldn't count on it.

Freddy and Caroline enter L. Both are dressed and Caroline is glowering

Freddy (*uncertainly*) Brad said you wanted to see us. Is everything all right?

Edith (*coldly*) No, it isn't. Someone entered Rom's bedroom last night and removed his body.

Freddy (*staring at her*) You're not *serious*? You don't *mean* that?

Edith I'm not in the habit of saying things I don't mean, Mr Bostock. Rom's body is missing, and so is Tanya Mason's. (*She glares at Caroline*)

Caroline (*sharply*) Well don't look at me. *I* haven't touched them. (*She pushes past Freddy to sit on the settee*)

Freddy (*to Douglas; puzzled*) Why would anyone move them?

Douglas I think we can hazard a guess, Freddy. But what we *really* need to know is where they were moved *to*. We've got to find them before the police arrive or all hell's going to break loose.

Stella and Lynda enter L, followed by Brad

Lynda What's wrong? Has something happened?

Caroline Someone's cleared off with the late unlamented.

Lynda and Stella react

(*Sweetly*) Better empty your handbags darlings, otherwise the Wicked Witch is going to search us all.

Bradford (*sharply*) Give it a rest, Caroline. This is serious.

Caroline glowers at him, rises, and crosses to the fireplace, her lips a thin line

Douglas (*heavily*) As Miss Clavers has just said, both Rom and Tanya's bodies have vanished. Before anyone sits down to breakfast, I want this house searched from top to bottom—attics to cellar, and if there's any objections, I'd like to hear them now.

All but Caroline mutter agreement

Then we're all agreed?

Caroline (*firmly*) Sorry to disappoint you, but the last thing *I* intend doing is tramping about this place looking for missing corpses. I'm staying right here. (*She looks at them defiantly*)

There is a short silence

Bradford Where do we start, then? Upstairs, downstairs, or in my lady's chamber?

Douglas It might be better if we pair off. Lynda and I'll do the attics. You and Edith the bedrooms, and Freddy and Stella the cellars.

Edith What about *this* floor?

Douglas We'll cover that when we've done the rest of the place. (*He glances around at them*) Is everyone ready?

All but Caroline give assent

Right. Then we'll meet back here as soon as possible.

Douglas leads the way out of the room, L, *followed by the others*

Bringing up the rear, Stella hesitates and looks back

Stella (*sincerely*) I'm sorry about what happened last night. You'd have been marvellous as Zoe. I thought it was a perfect piece of casting.

Caroline Oh? (*Sweetly*) I hadn't realized we had a casting expert in our midst. How exciting for us.

Stella (*stung*) There's no need to be rude. I was only trying to be friendly.

Caroline (*forcibly*) I don't *need* friends. I need *work*. And after what's happened here, I probably won't even be allowed to buy a ticket at a box office, let alone tread the boards.

Stella You're not the only one, you know. The rest of us aren't going to find it easy, either.

Freddy enters, and moves slightly L, *waiting for Stella*

Caroline (*glaring at him*) I don't give a *damn* about the rest of you. The only one *I'm* concerned about is me. Caroline Clavers.

Stella (*coldly*) Yes. I think that's *perfectly* obvious. (*She turns her head to see Freddy almost beside her*) Sorry to have kept you, Freddy. I was just trying to——(*She stops and looks at Freddy as though seeing him for the first time*)

Freddy Yes? (*Frowning*) Stella? (*Concerned*) Stella?

Stella (*dazedly*) I *was* right. He *was* murdered. (*Numbly*) And I know who did it. I know who killed Tanya and Rom.

She moves down L *and sinks on to the settee. They stare at her*

Caroline What do you mean . . . you *know* who killed them?

Stella (*still dazed*) I'd better start at the beginning, hadn't I? It was last night, you see . . . after Mr Marsh died. Listening to the discussion later on, it seemed perfectly obvious to *me* that *he* was the intended victim all along and Tanya's murder was a spur of the moment thing. I spent half the night trying to make sense of it all, but it was no use. Those newspaper cuttings, for instance. Why should anyone start sending them *now*? It's thirty years since Mabel Monk killed herself. And then there was Tanya's conviction that Mabel's mother, sister, or child was right here in the house.

Freddy (*nodding*) Yes. It does take some believing. But she *did* go looking for someone. They were quite sure about that.

Stella I know. But Mrs Bales said Tanya had asked her if she knew where *I* was and that didn't make sense to me. I was too young to be Mabel's mother or sister, and even if I'd been Mabel's *daughter*, Tanya couldn't have recognized me. She'd never seen the child in her life. No-one had. No. If she'd gone looking for anyone, it could only have been Mabel's *sister* . . . there's no-one here old enough to be her mother, is there? And if that were the case, it took me a step nearer to finding out who the murderer was.

Freddy How's that?

Stella Simple. Only two people qualified for the position of the sister. Lynda Molloy or Mrs Bales herself. But I'd known Lynda for *years*, so Mrs Bales had given herself away with a single stupid lie.

Freddy But . . . she hadn't. I mean . . . Tanya *was* looking for you. I told you last night. Remember? She came to my room to see if we were going through lines together.

Stella I know. And that's what started me wondering if *you* were lying too.

Freddy (*startled*) Me?

Stella (*calmly*) Oh, yes. You'd both told the same story and I was already convinced Mrs Bales was lying. Perhaps you were in it together? You could be Mabel Monk's *son*.

Freddy What?

Stella But then I remembered something. Something that cleared you. You told us you were in the shower when Tanya came looking for me, and when I went back to my room after borrowing Lynda's script, I noticed the carpet outside your door was wet. You must have been dripping all over it as you spoke to her.

Freddy (*relieved*) I was. And that corridor wasn't the warmest place I'd ever stood in with only a towel tied round me.

Stella So if *you* were telling the truth, then so was Mrs Bales. Tanya *had* been looking for me. But why? It was this morning before it struck me. The first time she'd seen me, I was dressed up to look like Mabel Monk. And who was responsible for that? *Lynda* of course . . . my second suspect and a self-confessed Mabel worshipper. If Tanya *was* looking for me, it could only have been to question me about my involvement with her. Much as I hated to admit it, it now looked as though Lynda had killed her. But I was wrong again. She *couldn't* have done it. While Tanya was upstairs looking for me, Lynda was down here talking to Rom and the others. I felt so frustrated, I could have screamed.

Caroline (*tightly*) That's nothing to the frustration *I'm* feeling right now. Are you going to tell us who killed the bloody woman or aren't you?

Stella I'm almost finished. It was *you* who finally put me on the right track.

Caroline (*surprised*) Me?

Stella Just now. You were standing in exactly the same place as Tanya was last night when I walked in wearing that awful gown. I was looking straight at her when the commotion began, and remember wondering if there was something wrong with her eyes. They didn't seem to be focused on me at all, you see . . . and of course, they *weren't*. I've only just realized it. She hardly noticed me. She was looking at the person on my left . . . just as *you* were a few minutes ago when Freddy came in.

Freddy (*puzzled*) So?

Stella Don't you see? It wasn't *me* who startled Tanya . . . it was the sight of someone she never expected to see here in a million years. Mabel Monk's sister . . . Mrs Bales, the housekeeper.

They look at her in amazement

Freddy (*protesting*) But you just said . . . (*Dazedly*) Mrs *Bales*?

Stella For thirty years she's blamed Romney Marsh for her sister's suicide, but it's taken her this long to be able to do anything about it. It wasn't until his previous housekeeper retired last year that she saw her chance. She applied for, and got, the job of housekeeper to him and from that day on, she's been planning to make him pay for what he did. It was incredible bad luck for her that Tanya was in the cast and recognized her. Possibly the only person in the world who could have connected her with Mabel. You can imagine how frantic she must have been. If Tanya opened her mouth, there'd never be another chance to get near him.

Freddy (*thoughtfully*) I'm not saying you're wrong, but surely . . . well . . . if she'd been with him all that time, why didn't she kill him earlier? She had plenty of opportunity.

Stella (*shaking her head*) I don't know. Perhaps yesterday was some kind of appropriate anniversary. Mabel's birthday . . . or the day she died.

Freddy Yes . . . but why wait all day to do it? If there was a chance that Tanya might recognize her, why didn't she get it over with before any of us even arrived.

Caroline I think *I* can answer that. Phillipa Jordan was the original choice for Lady Millicent. Douggie mentioned it yesterday. But she couldn't do it and Tanya was brought in as a last-minute replacement. The Bales woman wouldn't have known about it until she arrived here.

Stella So as I was saying . . . if she wanted to continue with her plan, she had no other choice but to kill Tanya, too. I imagine she waited on the landing till she saw her making her way downstairs again, killed her, and dragged her into the room next door while we were all in here talking. From then on, it all went according to plan. As his housekeeper, she had plenty of opportunity to fill one of his chocolates with poison and slip it into the box while we were having dinner. It was only a matter of time, then, before he ate it and died.

Freddy (*stunned*) Oh, my God. I was eating them, too. She could have killed *me*. (*He sits in shock*)

Caroline But how did she expect to get away with it?

Stella I don't suppose she did. She only killed Tanya to prevent her giving a warning. Now she's achieved her purpose, I don't think she'll be particularly worried about *what* happens to her. I got the distinct impression that having to murder Tanya really upset her.

Freddy Look . . . I can't take all this in. I thought *I* dreamed up some pretty weird characters, but this is too fantastic for words. (*Standing*) I vote we get her in here and see what she has to say for herself.

Stella I'd rather the others were here first.

Freddy OK. I'll go tell her we're having a meeting and want her in on it. Then you can keep an eye on her while I find the rest of them. Agreed?

Without waiting for an answer he exits L

Caroline (*after a slight pause*) I suppose I owe you an apology. I know I'm a bitch at times, but you've got to protect yourself in this business. Let them see you've got feelings and they'll trample all over you.

Stella Who will?

Caroline Them. Managements. Everybody else who's trying to claw their way up the ladder. (*Bitterly*) Trust none of them, that's my motto.

Stella (*quietly*) You sound as though you've had some bad experiences.

Caroline (*shrugging*) Some. But nothing as freaky as this. When my agent put me up for it, he warned me about Marsh and his I-am-God attitude, but I thought I could handle it. No fading star was going to get *me* jumping through hoops, I told him. Try his tricks on me and he'd soon find out he'd bitten off more than he could chew. (*Laughing harshly*) Talk about self delusion. If things hadn't turned out the way they did, I'd have been in a straight-jacket and padded cell before opening night. Why no-one tried to bump him off before, I can't imagine. Can you cook?

Stella stares at her blankly

Stella (*nodding*) Yes.

Caroline Good. Then we're not likely to starve to death, are we? I can't boil *water* without burning it.

Stella still looks blank

(*Patiently*) If you're right about the Bales woman, we can hardly let her go on doing the catering, can we? She might slip a dose of rat poison or something into the soup and get rid of all of us.

Stella (*smiling sadly*) That's not very likely. She's done what she wanted to do, and the rest of us won't concern her in the least.

Caroline Don't fool yourself. No matter how cracked they are, self-preservation comes high on anybody's list. Once she knows we're on to her, she's not going to sit quietly waiting for the police to arrive. We'll have to lock her in her room and fend for ourselves. (*Rising*) And speaking of fending ... I suppose we'd better make our own arrangements for breakfast?

Stella I don't know. She *was* preparing it.

Caroline Yes. But knowing what we know now, I'd rather take *my* chances with toast and coffee. (*She glances at the door* L) What was that?

Stella (*puzzled*) What?

Caroline That noise. As though someone had knocked something over.

Stella I didn't hear anything. Maybe it came from upstairs?

Caroline (*frowning*) Do you think he's having trouble with her? They should have been back here by now.

Stella It's only been a minute or so.

Caroline All the same ... (*Impulsively*) I think I'll go see what's happening.

Stella (*rising*) Shall I come with you?

Caroline (*shaking her head*) I'll be back in a second.

She exits L

Stella gazes after her, then turns away and wanders over to the window, staring out into the fog. After a few minutes she turns her head and glances at the door L, *again. Biting her lip, she suddenly moves towards it. As she does so, Caroline screams loudly, off* L. *Stella halts in her tracks staring down the hall until* . . .

Caroline stumbles blindly into the room

Stella (*afraid*) What is it? What's wrong? (*She seizes hold of her*)
Caroline They're dead. Both of them. There on the kitchen floor. There's blood all over. They've been murdered. (*She clings desperately to Stella*)

CURTAIN

SCENE 2

The same. Twenty minutes later

Douglas is standing by the fireplace, deep in thought and a blood-spattered Freddy sits on the settee, head bowed, as Lynda gently sponges the back of his skull with a bloodstained pad. A bowl of warm water rests beside him

Freddy (*groaning*) Oww.
Lynda (*shakily*) You should really be seeing a doctor. There's a lump the size of an egg, *and* a nasty looking graze. (*She puts the cloth into the bowl with distaste*)
Douglas (*to Freddy*) You're absolutely *certain* you didn't see who hit you?
Freddy (*weakly*) I've already told you. I didn't see *anything*. I went into the kitchen, and there she was, sprawled out by the sink . . . blood all over the place. I went over to see if she really *was* dead and just as I bent over her, the roof caved in. (*He fingers his wound gingerly*)
Lynda Caroline thought *you* were dead too. It gave her a terrible shock. (*She picks up the bowl and puts it on the table behind the settee*)
Freddy It didn't do much for *me*. (*He winces in pain*)
Douglas Let's go over it again. Just in case we've missed something. How long were you in here before you went looking for Mrs Bales? Five minutes? Ten?
Freddy (*groaning*) I don't *know*. Stella was telling us how she'd worked out the Bales woman had done it. Maybe ten.
Douglas (*nodding*) All right. Now Lynda and I were searching the attics, Brad and Edith the bedrooms. Caroline, Stella and yourself were in here . . . so who murdered Mrs Bales and cracked you over the head? There's no-one else in the house. (*Biting his lip*) Damn it. The more I go over it, the more unreal it gets. I've said it before and I'll say it again . . . the whole thing smacks of theatrical trickery. Multiple murder . . . vanishing bodies . . . no-one able to go for help because of killer dogs, and a blanket of fog so thick, you can't see your nose in front of your face . . .
Freddy (*disconsolately*) Special effects working overtime.
Douglas Exactly. (*Suddenly he stares at him*) That's it. *Special effects.*

They look at him blankly

(*Excitedly*) Stay here. Stay right here. Don't move and keep your eyes open. (*He hurries towards the door* L)

Lynda (*startled*) Where are you going?

There is no reply as he exits

Lynda gazes after him in bewilderment

Freddy (*clutching his wound*) Have another look at this, will you? It's starting to make me feel really sick and those tablets are doing no good at all. She must have hit me with a building brick.

Lynda She? (*She turns to look at him*)

He looks at her blankly

You said "she".

Freddy (*slowly realizing*) That's *right*. It was a *woman*.

Lynda But if you didn't see anyone ... ?

Freddy I know. I know. (*Struggling to remember*) There was *perfume*. I got a whiff of it before I blacked out. A sort of heavy ... orange smell.

Lynda Orange? (*She looks puzzled*) Are you *sure*? That's the sort of thing Tanya used. She's worn it for years. It was specially created for her in France. She was wearing it last night at dinner.

Freddy Well that's what it was. I'd recognize it anywhere.

Edith enters L. *She is now dressed*

Edith Is it really necessary to keep using this room? After what happened in here, I'd have thought one of the others far more comfortable.

Lynda The way people are dying around here, it doesn't seem to matter *where* we gather. How's Caroline?

Edith A trifle more rational than she was twenty minutes ago, but I've left Miss Bakewell with her just in case. (*To Freddy*) And how are *you* feeling?

Freddy (*forcing a smile*) I'll live. (*He closes his eyes and his head sags*)

Bradford Kyle enters L

Edith (*giving him an odd look*) Where's Douggie? I have to speak to him.

Lynda I don't know. We were in here talking when suddenly he upped and shot out as though the place were on fire. It was something Freddy said that started him off. Something about special effects.

Bradford (*thoughtfully*) Special effects, eh? Can't say they've any particular significance for me. Rom was the man for that. He knew more about that side of things than anybody I know. Remember that scene in *Forest of Eyes* where he changed into the Werewolf? He thought that one out himself ... beginning to end.

Lynda Do I ever. It scared the living daylights out of me ... and I was in my twenties at the time. That scene where he followed the girl through the trees and the fog was swirling round them. (*She shudders*) Ugh.

Bradford (*looking at the window*) And speaking of fog ... Looks like it's starting to lift.

Everyone looks at the windows

Edith (*relieved*) He's right. I can see the trees at the edge of the moat. (*She moves closer*) And the curve of the drive.

Freddy What about the dogs?

Bradford (*looking*) Not a sign. But they could be anywhere. Maybe round the back. (*Puzzled*) This is stupid.

Lynda What is?

Bradford The way it's clearing. I've never seen fog lift *this* quickly. It's like something out of——(*He stops and bangs his clenched fist against his forehead*) Idiot. Why didn't I think of it before? (*To the others*) Special effects. *Fog machines.*

Freddy What? (*He looks at Bradford in a puzzled manner*)

Bradford (*moving* DL) Fog machines. He had studio fog machines built into the house. A flick of a switch and bingo . . . instant fog.

Lynda But that's ridiculous.

Bradford Is it? Any more ridiculous than doing up this place to look like the House of Usher, complete with fake torture chambers and imitation graveyard? It's all *set dressing*. Reality wasn't good enough for Rom. He wanted to live in a world of pure fantasy. Oh, the man was a genius at the things he did, but he'd had a slate loose for years. Who else would fill a moat with damn piranha fish? It must have been costing him a fortune to keep them alive.

Edith (*coldly*) Not in the least. For your information——(*She breaks off*)

Douglas enters L, *slightly breathless and triumphant*

Douglas I was right, wasn't I? No power . . . no fog.

Bradford Spot on, Douggie. Now if only those blasted hounds could be turned off by the same method, we could all slip away into the night and leave the *police* to sort the whole damn mess out.

Lynda (*surprised*) We couldn't do *that.*

Bradford Why not? With Rom *and* his housekeeper dead, who's to say we were here at all?

Edith Aren't you forgetting the *gatekeeper*? He had a list of all the expected guests this weekend. And I'm sure he couldn't fail to remember *your* turning up out of the blue. Besides . . . I'm not going anywhere till I find out what's happened to Rom's body.

Freddy (*standing shakily*) Excuse me . . . I'm . . . not feeling too well.

Lynda (*anxiously*) Freddy . . . (*She moves to help him*)

Freddy (*weakly*) Need to go to the bathroom. (*He clutches feebly at Lynda*)

Lynda (*anxiously*) It's that bang on the head. I knew he needed a doctor. I *said* so, didn't I?

Douglas (*moving to Freddy*) It's all right, Lynda. I'll take him.

Freddy (*mumbling*) Just dizzy, that's all. And cold. Nothing to worry about. (*His legs begin to buckle*)

Douglas (*catching him*) Easy does it. (*He puts Freddy's arm around his shoulder and supports him*) Somebody give me a hand to get him upstairs.

Bradford takes Freddy's other arm

Lynda (*stricken*) Oh, God. *He's* not going to die, too, is he?

Bradford (*sharply*) Of course he's not. It's concussion, that's all. He'll be fine ... providing he's kept warm and quiet.

Edith There are spare blankets on the other bed in *my* room. I'll get them for you.

Douglas It's all right, Edith. We'll manage. You stay with Lynda. I'd rather no-one be left alone from now on.

Douglas and Bradford move towards the door L, *supporting a stumbling Freddy*

Freddy (*mumbling*) Sorry. Be all right. Just help me up the stairs.

They exit ...

... leaving Edith and Lynda gazing after them. After a moment, Edith turns

Edith I think I'll make some coffee. Would you care for a cup?

Lynda (*shaking her head*) A good stiff brandy's what I really need.

Edith (*off-handedly*) You know where it is. (*She turns to exit then pauses*) By the way ... when you were searching the attics ... did you ever lose sight of Douglas?

Lynda (*frowning*) Maybe for a second or two, but no longer. Why? (*Realizing*) You don't think *he* ...

Edith Of course not. I just wanted to be sure. I already *know* who killed Mrs Bales and attacked Mr Bostock, but I need to be sure of my facts before I present my conclusions to the police.

Lynda (*staring at her*) Who is it?

Edith It doesn't take a lot of working out. Think it over while I'm making my coffee. You'll be surprised you didn't see it before.

Edith exits L

Lynda sinks on to the settee, a puzzled expression on her face. She is obviously trying to work out the solution. After a moment, her eyes widen

Lynda No. (*She rises and moves distractedly around the room*) It all fits. But why? *Why?*

Stella enters L

Stella Why what?

Lynda (*turning and seeing her*) The murderer. It's *Brad.* He's the only one it *could* have been. Listen.

She draws Stella to the settee and they sit

We'll begin with the newspaper clippings. Obviously Mrs Bales would never have been able to get up to London on a daily basis to send them. She had to have an accomplice there ... and that was Brad.

Stella But I thought you said he'd been in Paris?

Lynda I know. That's what he told us, but it was a lie. He'd never been anywhere near France. *He* posted the clippings, one each day, building up to the date when Mrs Bales would poison Rom with one of his own

chocolates . . . but because Rom suddenly invited the rest of us down here
for the weekend, it completely upset their plan. As soon as Mrs Bales got
to know we were coming, she must have called Brad and told him.
Between them, they decided he'd better gatecrash the party by pretending
he was angling for a part, and they'd go ahead with the murder but try to
blame it on one of us. Of course, what neither of them knew, was that
Tanya had replaced Phillipa Jordan as Lady Millicent . . . and when she
recognized Mrs Bales, they had no choice but to kill her as well. Then
later on, when Brad found out you'd realized who Mrs Bales really was,
he had to kill *her* to stop her from giving him away. It was pure bad luck
that Freddy walked in on him, just as he'd done it, but luckily he managed
to knock him out with something and get back upstairs to pretend to help
Edith look for the missing bodies. You see?

Stella (*puzzled*) But how did he know I'd realized who Mrs Bales was? He
wasn't even in the room when I told Freddy and Caroline.

Lynda Maybe he was listening at the door? What's it matter? Now we *know*
he's the murderer, what are we going to do about it?

Stella (*after a moment*) We'll have to tell the others.

Lynda (*nodding*) Of course. (*Rising*) The only thing that *does* still puzzle me
is what the link is between Brad and Mrs Bales. I mean . . . he couldn't
have had a "thing" for her, could he? He's as gay as they come.

Stella (*thinking about it*) It's possible. There *are* married gays.

Bradford enters L, *behind them*

Bradford That's right, dear hearts. There are black sheep in *every* family.
(*Interested*) Who are we talking about, by the way? Anyone I know?

Lynda (*taking a deep breath and turning to him*) As a matter of fact, Brad . . .
we were talking about *you*.

Bradford (*raising an eyebrow*) My favourite subject. And what were you
saying about me? Something flattering, I hope?

Lynda No. It wasn't flattery, Brad. Far from it. (*She hesitates*) We *know*,
you see. We know it was you who killed Tanya and the others.

Bradford (*after a moment*) Oh. (*He looks from one to the other*) I see. (*He
moves round the settee and sits on the* R *arm*) And would it be too
inquisitive of me to ask how you . . . er . . . ?

Lynda Edith told me. A few minutes ago.

Bradford (*understanding*) Ah.

Lynda She didn't accuse you *outright*. She just put me on the right track. It
was killing Mrs Bales that gave you away. You see . . . Douggie and I were
up in the attic when it happened . . . and we never lost sight of each other,
so that cleared us. Caroline, Stella and Freddy were in here, so that put
them out of the running, leaving only you and Edith as the possible
murderer.

Bradford (*easily*) And why couldn't Edith be the murderer?

Lynda Because when Tanya was killed, she was in here with Douggie and
Rom. When *you* came in with blood all over your hand, it wasn't from the
stair-rail, as you told us, it was the blood that came from Tanya when you
killed her.

Bradford (*thoughtfully*) Hmm. But I seem to remember Freddy managing to get it on *his* hand too.

Lynda Hardly surprising. You've always paid attention to detail, Brad. Once you realized you'd got the blood on you and didn't have time to change, you smeared the stair-rail with it to support the story you told us. It was almost inevitable someone else would brush against it.

Bradford Well, well, well. What a pity you're not an actress and a few years older, Lyn. You'd make a first-class Miss Marple. (*He rises*)

Stella (*watching him carefully*) You're not going to deny it?

Bradford (*thinking for a moment*) No. I don't think so. You seem to have covered all bases, as they say in the States.

Lynda But *why*, Brad? Why did you *do* it? You're not the murdering type. I've known you for years. Oh, I wouldn't trust you as far as I could throw you with a roomful of chorus boys, but murder . . .

Bradford (*smiling*) What's it matter? If the police see it the way you do, then it looks like I'm done for. They'll have me behind bars before you can say "Bum". Poor old Brad. (*Curious*) You *are* going to tell them all this I suppose?

Lynda (*quietly*) I'm sorry. But they'd have come to the same conclusion themselves eventually.

Bradford (*thoughtfully*) Yes. I suppose they would. (*He turns to exit*)

Lynda Where are you going?

Bradford Oh . . . nowhere in particular. Can't go far anyway, can I? I'll probably go upstairs. There's . . . something I have to do.

Bradford exits L

There is a short silence

Stella Lynda . . . We're not wrong, are we? I mean . . . we're quite sure it's Brad?

Lynda (*puzzled*) Of course we are. He admitted it, didn't he?

Stella Not *exactly*. He just didn't deny it.

Lynda It's the same thing. (*She sits in the easy chair* R)

Stella No. It isn't. And there's something else, too. Something I said earlier . . . (*Thinking*) If only I could remember what it *was*. (*Sighing*) I'm sorry. I'm still not convinced that Brad's the one we're looking for.

Lynda (*incredulous*) But who else could it be?

Edith enters L

Stella (*not seeing her*) Edith.

Edith What about me? (*She moves* C)

Stella (*steadily*) I was saying that *you* could have killed Mrs Bales just as easily as Brad could.

Edith (*scornfully*) Don't be ridiculous. I practically saw the man do it.

Stella We've only your word for that, Edith.

Edith And the evidence of your own eyes. Look at me. When Brad and I set out to search the bedrooms, I was still in my nightclothes. I went into my room to dress whilst he began checking the rooms. He was out of my sight for at least ten minutes. Plenty of time for him to come down here, kill Mrs Bales and attack Freddy, then return upstairs to resume searching.

Stella But the same reasoning applies to yourself, Edith. For ten minutes, *you* were out of *his* sight.

Edith Have you ever washed and dressed in less than ten minutes, Miss Bakewell?

Douglas and Caroline enter L. *Caroline looks shaken, but is in control of herself. She moves round the settee* L, *and sits next to Stella*

Douglas Where's Brad?

Lynda I . . . think he went upstairs . . .

Douglas But I told him to come down here. There's some serious talking to do.

Edith I don't think there's any need for that now, Douggie. *Brad* killed Tanya and Mrs Bales.

Douglas (*startled*) What? (*He glances at the others*)

Edith He came down here while I was dressing, killed Mrs Bales, knocked out Mr Bostock, then hurried back upstairs in time to meet me coming out of my room.

Douglas (*dazed*) Are you *sure* about this, Edith?

Edith Of course. There isn't a shadow of doubt about it. The question is, what are we going to do about him? He's obviously got to be restrained until the police arrive.

Douglas (*hesitating*) I don't know. If you really think Brad *is* responsible, it might be an idea to have him down here and face him with it. At least give him a chance to defend himself.

Lynda We've already done that. Just before you came in.

Douglas And what did he say?

Lynda (*reluctantly*) He admitted it.

Stella (*standing*) He didn't admit *anything*. And the reason for that is because he didn't do it.

Edith Then who did?

Stella (*defeated*) I don't know. (*She turns alway and moves* DL)

Freddy enters L, *carrying a small bottle of perfume. He is unsteady and his face is drawn*

Freddy But I do.

Everybody turns in surprise

Lynda Freddy . . .

Douglas (*moving to him*) I thought you were asleep.

Freddy I was. But something woke me. (*To Edith*) Can you guess what it was, Edith?

Edith How should *I* know?

Freddy It was the smell of oranges. Coming from the blankets Douggie threw over me. Blankets borrowed from *your* room.

Douglas What? (*To Freddy*) Just a minute, Freddy . . .

Freddy (*ignoring him*) There was only one person here this weekend who wore orange-scented perfume, and she's dead. But the person who tried to brain me in the kitchen was wearing the same perfume . . . I remembered smelling it, later . . . so what was it doing on your blankets?

Edith (*puzzled and indignant*) I've no idea.

Douglas Freddy . . .

Freddy I've nearly done. (*Leaning on the table*) I hauled myself off the bed and managed to make it across the corridor to your room. (*He holds up the perfume bottle*) I found *this* in your make-up case. "L'orange". Specially created for Tanya Mason by Jeanmaire of Paris. (*He closes his eyes and his head sags*)

Stella hurries to him and supports him

Edith (*standing*) I've never set eyes on that bottle in my life . . . and how *dare* you go searching through my things?

Stella (*to Freddy*) You're perspiring like mad. You shouldn't be on your feet at all. Here. Sit on the settee. (*She leads him around* R *to seat him*)

Freddy (*protesting weakly*) I'm all right. Really I am. (*He sits*)

Edith Did you hear what I said? I demand an apology.

Caroline (*glaring at her*) Leave him alone, can't you? You can see he's sick? And if you don't mind me saying so, I think it's *you* who should be doing the explaining.

Edith (*firmly*) There's no explanation necessary.

Douglas But I think there is, Edith. None of this is making the slightest bit of sense.

Caroline Maybe not to you, but it is to *me*. It's as clear as daylight. She and the Bales woman were in it together. The Bales woman killed Tanya Mason, and *she* (*indicating Edith*) poisoned Marsh, murdered her *partner* and tried to brain *him*. (*She indicates Freddy*) That tarty scent's given the whole thing away. (*She glares at Edith*)

Douglas (*shaking his head*) No. That's not the way it was, at all. What I was trying to say earlier, is that those blankets *didn't* come from Edith's room. They came from *Stella's*.

There is a stunned silence

Stella Mine?

Douglas That's why I said none of this made sense. Edith *offered* her blankets, but when we got Freddy upstairs, there didn't seem much point in going all down the corridor to get then when Stella's room was next door and there was a spare set in there. So while Brad got him into bed, I went round there and grabbed them.

Lynda So how did Tanya's perfume get on to Stella's blankets?

Stella I've no idea. (*Remembering*) Unless she went into my room last night . . . when she was looking for me.

Caroline She'd hardly be spraying perfume about, would she? And even if she had been . . . you'd have noticed it the minute you walked in.

Stella That's right . . . and I didn't smell *anything*.

Freddy (*opening his eyes*) You couldn't have missed this. It's quite powerful.

Douglas Then if Stella didn't notice it, it must have been sprayed there

recently. This morning. To make it appear as though *Stella* had attacked
Freddy and killed Mrs Bales.

Lynda But she couldn't have done. We all know Stella and Caroline were
together when that happened. And how could anyone know Freddy had
smelled perfume when he was attacked? He'd forgotten it himself until a
quarter of an hour ago. In fact, I'm the only other one who knew about it.
There was no-one else here when he told me.

Caroline Then how did the bottle get into *her* make-up case? (*She looks at
Edith*)

Edith I think that's patently obvious. Someone intended me to take the
blame.

Lynda For *what*? It was the sheerest chance that Freddy recognized the
perfume and went looking for it. It shouldn't have meant anything to the
rest of you.

Freddy (*attempting to sit up*) She's right. It shouldn't. (*He thinks*) Unless . . .
(*He looks round*) Where's Brad?

Lynda Upstairs. Why?

Freddy We'd better have him down here. I may be wrong, but I think the
last piece of the puzzle's just dropped into place.

Stella You mean . . . you know who the murderer is?

Freddy (*slowly*) Yes. I think I *do*.

Everyone looks at each other

Douglas I'll go fetch him.

Douglas exits L.

Caroline (*to Freddy*) Who is it?

Lynda Yes. Who?

Freddy I'll tell you everything when Brad's here. (*He feels his head again and
smiles wanly*) You'd better make yourselves comfortable. It's a bit
involved and I might tend to wander in my present condition. But all the
same, I'm sure I can tie the loose ends together now.

Stella remains standing, but the rest seat themselves

It was the perfume that gave me the final clue. If it hadn't been for that,
our killer might have got away scot-free.

Lynda (*baffled*) But what's that got to do with it?

Freddy (*smiling faintly*) Absolutely nothing. At least . . . not with the actual
murders. It was a red herring. Something to throw us off the scent. (*He
winces*) Sorry . . . no pun intended. But I'll explain in a minute.

Caroline (*irritated*) It's like something out of one of those awful Agatha
Christie plays. Everyone gathered in the library to hear the great detective
tell them how wonderful he is.

Freddy (*tiredly*) There's nothing of the great detective about me, I'm afraid.
I put it all together by trial and error. Most of it, you already know. How
this whole thing seems to be tied in with Mabel Monk and how Mrs Bales
appears to have taken the job here simply to kill Rom for what he'd done
to her sister.

Edith Which is something I find myself totally unable to accept. Rom did nothing that *any* decent man wouldn't have done in the same circumstances.

Freddy Be that as it may ... without a body to perform an autopsy on, we'll never find out *what* killed him. Poison *or* heart attack.

Stella But the police are sure to find him ... even if *we* can't. It's not that easy to hide a body.

Freddy *Two* bodies ... and in *this* instance, you're wrong. "Usher"'s the perfect place to dispose of an unwanted body. Most people would have carp or trout in a moat that went round their house. What did Rom have?

Lynda (*realizing*) Oh, my God. The piranha.

Freddy Exactly. And thanks to Rom's eccentricity, he provided the murderer with a perfect way of concealing the corpses. If they drag the moat now, they'll probably find the bones, but not much else.

As the realization sinks in, Edith rises unsteadily and stumbles to the windows. Quickly opening them, she steps on to the balcony and looks downwards into the water. As the rest of them think their own thoughts ...

Douglas enters L, *looking shaken*

Lynda (*noticing him*) Where's Brad?

Douglas He won't be down. He's killed himself.

There is a shocked reaction

I found him in his bathroom. The knife's still in his hand. (*He moves* L *and speaks to Freddy*) Was he the one you ...?

Freddy nods gently. Edith moves back into the room with a look of stone on her face, leaving the window open. She moves L *to remain standing by the desk, eyes unfocused*

There was no note, but obviously he killed himself rather than face a trial. (*To Freddy*) How did you know?

Freddy (*tiredly*) I suppose I suspected him from the start. I never seriously thought of these as women's crimes. You know ... cutting throats and atacks from behind. That's the sort of thing I'd expect from a man. When Tanya died, Douggie was here in the room with Edith, so that seemed to indicate Brad was the one who killed her. Then came the problem of the missing bodies. Again, I couldn't see a women carrying them far, so I had to assume a man did it. Of course ... this time, it could have been Brad or *you*. Later on though, when Mrs Bales was killed and someone tried to crack my skull open ... for a time I thought I'd been wrong and the killer *was* a woman. I mean ... what man wears perfume? (*He pauses*) When I passed out and came round with the smell of Tanya's perfume in my nostrils, I suspected Edith because I thought the blankets belonged to her ... and what's more, I found the bottle inside her make-up case. But a few minutes ago I began to see daylight.

Douglas Yes?

Freddy Obviously I can't swear to this, but Brad must have overheard my conversation with Lynda, and when I was taken ill, saw a chance to use

Tanya's perfume to frame Edith. When Douggie went for the blankets to tuck me up, Brad got the bottle of perfume out and after Douggie went off to see Caroline, thinking the blankets were Edith's, gave them a light dousing of it, then hid the bottle in her make-ups case. There was no way I could miss smelling it when I woke up, and it would be easy to "jog my memory" and connect it with my attacker and Mrs Bales' murderer at an opportune moment.

Lynda (*slowly*) But as things turned out, he was too clever for his own good. The blankets weren't Edith's at all ... they were Stella's. Yet the bottle was still found in Edith's bag.

Freddy (*closing his eyes*) It was his only mistake.

There is a thoughtful silence

Caroline And what was the connection between him and the Bales woman?

Douglas (*heavily*) That's something we'll never know. They could have been friends, lovers, anything ... but whatever it was, they'd been planning this for a long time. Of course, what neither of them expected was that Rom would have a pack of dogs roaming the grounds to stop anyone leaving, and Brad was stuck here with the rest of us.

Lynda Even so ... they went on with their plan to kill Rom.

Douglas What else could they do? They'd set everything up and after killing Tanya, they'd no choice in the matter.

Lynda (*shaking her head*) It's all so unbelievable.

There is another silence

Caroline (*standing*) Well I don't know about anyone else, but *I* could do with a drink. Anyone care to join me?

Douglas I don't normally indulge so early in the day, but perhaps a small whisky.

Caroline (*crossing to the drinks*) I can't tell you what a relief this is. Knowing it's all over and there's no-one can point a finger at us. The first thing I'm going to do when we get out of here, is take a nice long break with Adrian, then start doing the rounds again. (*She pours the drinks*) God ... whoever thought I'd be looking forward to learning lines again?

Stella I know. That's the worst part of——(*She stops*) *What* did you say?

Caroline (*puzzled*) Sorry?

Stella Just then. What did you say about learning lines?

Caroline (*faltering*) Whoever thought I'd be looking forward to learning lines.

Stella That's *it*. That's what he was trying to say.

Lynda Who was? What's wrong?

Stella (*dazedly*) Mr Marsh. Rom. That's what he was trying to say just before he died. It's what's been nagging at me for the past ten minutes or so. How did Tanya know I was upstairs learning Zoe's lines? She wasn't even in the room when he made the decision for me to take over the role. The only ones who knew about it were Rom, Mr Dekker, Edith, Freddy and me.

Caroline So?

Stella (*to Freddy*) But *you* said she came to your room to see if we were running over the lines together. Which means she already *knew* I was replacing Caroline.

Douglas (*frowning*) But she couldn't have done. The subject never came up. We were too concerned with the press cuttings.

Stella Then she couldn't possibly have gone to Freddy's room to look for me, could she? (*To Freddy again*) You were *lying*, weren't you, Freddy?

Freddy (*taken aback*) What?

Stella You've been lying all along. It was you who killed Tanya and Rom. And you who killed Mrs Bales.

Freddy Me? (*Laughing incredulously*) Why would *I* want to kill them?

Stella Because Mabel Monk was *your* mother.

Everyone looks at Freddy

Lynda Stella . . .

Stella Oh, it's only a guess on my part, but if it's true, it clears up something that's puzzled us all. Why did Mrs Bales wait thirty years to try and revenge herself on Romney Marsh? The answer is, of course, because she didn't know *how* to do it. They moved in different worlds. It would have been difficult, if not impossible for her to meet him on a social level, and as for getting close enough to kill him and escaping undetected . . . (*She shakes her head*) No. If she did have thoughts of revenge, I think she must have given them up a long time ago. There was the baby, you see, Mabel's baby. She had to look after *him*. I don't think there's any doubt she brought him up as her own son because the least hint she was caring for Mabel's missing baby, and the world's press would have been hammering on her door. As we all know, *that* never happened, so it's safe to assume that it's only during the last few years Freddy found out who his real mother was, and heard the circumstances surrounding his birth for the first time. That's when *he* decided to punish Rom for what had happened.

Freddy I don't *believe* this. Does she know what she's saying?

Stella When Rom's housekeeper retired last year, Mrs Bales applied for the job, while *he* began writing a play that couldn't fail to bring him to Rom's attention. On his own admission, he watched every film Rom had ever appeared in and made the character of Solomons so tempting, it couldn't fail to attract him. (*To Freddy*) There's not another actor in the world could play Solomons the way you wrote it for Romney Marsh.

Douglas (*nodding*) That's true. The minute I read it I knew it was a Marsh vehicle. There was no doubt about it.

Stella Which is why it was sent to you in the first place. You've been Rom's agent for over twenty years and as a producing management, couldn't fail to see the possibilities. (*To Freddy*) But things went wrong almost from the start, didn't they? Rom failed to react the way you thought he would and Tanya replaced Phillipa Jordan as Lady Millicent. When you found out she'd recognized Mrs Bales, you killed her while Mrs Bales pretended to look for her, giving *me* as an excuse. But as you ran upstairs afterwards, you managed to get blood on the banister rail, not to mention the carpet outside your room. That's why it was wet when I went by later, after borrowing Lynda's script. Not only had you been showering to get Tanya's blood off yourself, you'd been scrubbing it off the Axminster.

Freddy (*shaking his head*) And I thought I was the one with writer's imagination.

Stella Oh, you've got imagination all right, Freddy. And a lot of nerve. During the time you were eating Rom's chocolates, you managed to slip the poisoned one into the box. Mrs Bales must have had it ready for some time.

Freddy Then why didn't *she* kill him? She had plenty of opportunity.

Stella I think she was going to. But when you were suddenly included in the party he invited for the weekend, you had to change plans, and by the time you discovered that none of us could leave, it was too late to change them again. Rom ate the chocolate and died. During the night, you and Mrs Bales moved the bodies and dropped them into the moat. I must confess, I'd never given the piranha a second thought, but it made quite sure that no-one could examine the bodies for clues.

Freddy (*rising*) I'm not going to stay here and listen to this rubbish. If anyone wants me, I'll be in my room. (*He moves up* C)

Stella It's no use, Freddy. It's all over. Like a fool, I told you my suspicions about Mrs Bales, and you went off to the kitchen supposedly to bring her back here. Instead, you killed her in the same way you killed Tanya, then faked an attack on yourself by banging your head against the wall or something. That was the thump that Caroline heard. You weren't half as hurt as you made out to be. In fact, from then on, you had to be even more inventive because now there *was* a body for the police to examine and you couldn't dispose of that one so easily. By pretending you'd had a whiff of Tanya's perfume when your supposed attacker hit you, you opened a new trail. You faked a collapse and when Douggie and Brad put you to bed, you went to Tanya's room, took the bottle of perfume and sprayed it on to the blankets Douggie covered you with . . . thinking they were Edith's. Then you went over to *her* room to put the bottle in her make-up case.

Lynda But . . . why did *Brad* kill himself?

Stella He didn't. After we told him Edith had accused *him* of being the murderer, it's my belief he thought *she* was the killer and was trying to frame him. He probably went upstairs to have it out with her, walked in on Freddy arranging his "clue" and got himself killed.

Douglas (*protesting*) But he's in his *own* room, not Edith's.

Stella I don't doubt it. But I'm sure Freddy found *some* way of luring him back there before he killed him. *That's* why he was perspiring so heavily when he first came down . . . not because of his so-called concussion.

Freddy This is absolute tripe. (*Scornfully*) "Probably". "Possibly". "I think". You can't prove *any* of it.

Stella I know. But as soon as the police arrive, I'm sure *they'll* be able to. Forensic science is a marvellous thing. Skin particles . . . a stray hair . . . a speck of dust . . . it's amazing how much they can give away. And with *two* bodies to work on, there shouldn't be any difficulty in proving I'm right.

There is a silence

Freddy (*at last*) I really underestimated you, didn't I? It should have been *your* throat I slit.

Edith (*coming back to life*) So it *was* you. It *was* you who killed him. (*Her fingers close round the paper-knife*) The only man I've ever loved.

Freddy (*turning to face her*) Love? What do *you* know about love? He robbed me of my *mother*. (*Grinning*) Oh, yes . . . it was me who planned it all out. Harriet just did as I told her. She hated Marsh as much as I did, but she was too soft for her own good. When she realized Tanya had recognized her, she wanted to call the whole thing off, but I wasn't going to let a little thing like that stop *me*. I slit her throat without a second thought and dropped the poisoned chocolate into his box when no-one was looking. After we'd dumped the bodies in the moat, I thought we'd be safe, (*he glares at Stella*) but *she* started playing detectives and left me with no choice but to shut Harriet's mouth, too. If it hadn't been for *her* I'd have got away with it. (*Laughing*) What am I talking about? I *am* getting away with it. (*To Edith*) Out of the way. I'm leaving.

Edith brandishes the paper knife

(*Amused*) You're not going to try and stop me with *that*, are you?

Caroline Haven't you forgotten something? There's a pack of half-starved dogs roaming round outside. You'll never get to a car.

Douglas moves up to Edith and takes the knife from her, gently

Freddy Wouldn't I? Don't bet on it. You haven't heard much of them since last night, have you. (*He gives a short laugh*) I tossed a few pounds of doctored meat down to them early this morning. I don't somehow think they'll be in any condition to stop me by this time. (*To Edith*) I thought I told you to move.

Douglas points the knife at him

(*Amused*) Not you as well? You wouldn't know how.

Douglas Try me.

Edith (*icily*) Just for the record, Mr Bostock . . . you wouldn't have got away with it even if you *hadn't* killed Brad and Mrs Bales. You see . . . Those piranha in the moat. They all died during the summer. There's nothing in there now but weeds and a few frogs. The police would have recovered both bodies without any problem.

Freddy Well, well, well. We live and learn. (*He smiles*) But it doesn't matter now, does it? By this time tomorrow I'll be somewhere across the Atlantic. I booked my flight some days ago.

Douglas I don't think so, Freddy. We're going to put you under lock and key while one of us drives into the village to get the police.

Freddy Sorry to disappoint you, Douggie, but I can't afford to wait. (*He makes a sudden dash to the window and on to the balcony*) I'll drop you a postcard.

He vaults over the balustrade and vanishes from view

All rush forward to look

Stella (*agitated*) He's getting away.
Douglas I'll cut him off at the gates. (*He turns to exit* L)
Edith Wait. (*She clutches at his arm*)

A horrifying scream comes from below

Lynda (*looking down*) What's happening?
Caroline (*turning away*) Oh, my God. The piranha. They're eating him
   alive.
Douglas (*to Edith*) But you said they were *dead.*
Edith (*calmly*) I know. I lied.

*With a cruel smile on her face, she moves back into the room and sits. The
screams continue as everyone but Edith reacts to the scene below*

The CURTAIN *falls*

FURNITURE AND PROPERTY LIST

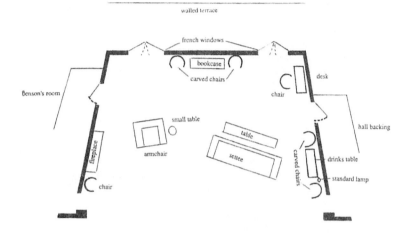

ACT I

SCENE 1

On stage: Bookcase. *On shelves:* first edition copies of books. *On top:* Chinese bowl and plates

2 carved chairs

Fireplace. *On hearth:* gothic fire irons, carved wooden fender. *By it:* bell-pull

Mantel shelf. *On it:* jar of spills, small oblong wooden box, photographs in miniature frames. *Above it:* huge oil painting, wall lamps

Carved high-back chair

Writing desk. *On it:* blotter, paper, envelopes, etc., paper-knife, table lamp. *On wall above:* small group of dark paintings. *By it:* internal wall telephone

Ladder-back chair

Oblong table. *On it:* large tray with various decanters including whisky, sherry, brandy, glasses. *On wall above:* framed portrait

Standard lamp

Carved chairs

Settee

Narrow table

Armchair

Small round table. *On it:* open box of chocolates, almost-empty sherry
    glass
Carpet
Window curtains (*open*)
Glass of whisky for **Edith**
Glass of sherry for **Caroline**
Glass of whisky for **Douglas**

Off stage: Tray with pot of tea, 2 cups, saucers, jug of milk, bowl of sugar, teaspoons
           (**Harriet**)

Personal: **Edith:** wrist-watch
         Caroline: diamond brooch and bracelet
         Freddy: spectacles (required throughout)
         Tanya: lots of jewellery
         Bradford: wrist-watch
         Romney: wrist-watch

SCENE 2

Strike: Dirty glasses
         Tray and tea things

Re-set: Window curtains closed

Set: *On table behind settee:* tray with coffee pot, sugar-bowl, cream jug, etc.
         Coffee cups and saucers on various surfaces
         Glass of brandy, play manuscript for **Romney**
         Pencil, manuscript for **Freddy**
         Manuscript for **Caroline**
         Manuscript, coffee cup for **Stella**
         Glasses of whisky for **Edith** and **Douglas**
         Brown envelope with 6 yellowing newspaper clippings in desk drawer

Off stage: Bloodstained handkerchief (**Bradford**)

Personal: As Scene 1

ACT II

SCENE 1

Strike: Envelope and clippings

Off stage: Handkerchief (**Harriet**)
           Mug of coffee (**Bradford**)

SCENE 2

Set: Bowl of water, cloth by settee

Off stage: Small bottle of perfume (**Freddy**)

LIGHTING PLOT

Practical fittings required: wall lamps, table lamp, standard lamp, central fitting

Interior. A drawing-room. The same scene throughout

ACT I, SCENE 1. Evening

To open: Dim general lighting, spectacular sunset effect outside

Cue 1	During Scene 1 *Gradually fade sunset effect outside and decrease lighting inside*	(Page 1)
Cue 2	**Edith** switches on central light *Snap on central light and increase general lighting*	(Page 2)

ACT I, SCENE 2. Evening

To open: General interior lighting, all practicals on

No cues

ACT II, SCENE 1. Early morning

Cue 3	**Harriet** opens curtains *Dull grey light—gradually increasing*	(Page 30)

ACT II, SCENE 2. Morning

To open: General interior lighting

No cues

EFFECTS PLOT

ACT I

Cue 1   **Edith:** "Is that clear?"   (Page 5)
        Telephone rings

Cue 2   **Freddy:** "... I saw the film once."   (Page 11)
        Begin fog effect outside, gradually increasing—continue till
          end of Scene 1

ACT II

Cue 3   As Scene 1 begins   (Page 30)
        Fog effect outside—continue until Cue 4

Cue 4   **Lynda:** "Something about Special Effects."   (Page 45)
        Begin to fade fog effect rapidly

Cue 5   **Edith:** "Wait." (*She clutches Douglas's arm*)   (Page 58)
        Horrifying scream from below—continue until Curtain

MADE AND PRINTED IN GREAT BRITAIN BY
LATIMER TREND & COMPANY LTD PLYMOUTH

MADE IN ENGLAND

Lightning Source UK Ltd.
Milton Keynes UK
UKHW022037300619
345292UK00005B/65/P